To my mother
CHERRY
who has always believed in me
and
to my first youth leaders
ARLEE AND LILY SCOTT
who always encourage me.

Acknowledgments

I have always been blessed by the encouragement and support of significant people in my life. My wife, Carol, has been a faithful partner on every major project I have undertaken. She has helped me reach publishing deadlines by picking up some of my other responsibilities, and she has tolerated my neglect of her during the writing of this manuscript.

The idea for this project came from Jane Vogel, Senior Editor of Youth and Children's Books at Victor Books. She has a heart for youth and sincerely wants to provide youth workers with the resources they need to increase their effectiveness with young people. She could have asked any number of professional counselors to write this book. I am grateful that she asked me. Appreciation is also expressed for the work of Randy Southern, SonPower editor, on the original manuscript.

Every therapist is surrounded by caring, competent professionals in the field. Several such professionals have served me as mentors, colleagues, and friends: Dr. Richard Bear, Dr. Keith Olson, Dr. Lydia Navarro, Dr. Albert Ringewald, Sandy Landstedt Thoma, Ronald Warren, Stan Beard, and Wayne Rice. They have shared their knowledge and expertise without reservation.

My son, Daniel, enabled me to actually experience what it is like for a parent to raise a teenager. I value my ongoing relationship with him. It is fulfilling to share in his growth as a young man.

Finally, I appreciate all of those teenagers who have allowed me to serve as their counselor. I have always felt honored by their trust. They have enriched my life in ways they will never know.

Contents

Preface

As a youth worker who counsels teenagers, you are a tremendous asset to any community. You voluntarily serve as a role model for our youth and you provide significant support to parents. You are in a unique position to influence the growth and development of emerging adults. Believe it or not, teenagers are likely to listen to you!

Several youth workers played meaningful parts in my life during my own teenage years. They gave me affirmation, their time and resources, and examples of adult maturity. By the time I graduated from high school, I wanted to be just like them. Following college, my wife and I had the privilege of serving as lay youth leaders in several churches during our young adult years.

Many youth workers have gained some understanding of the counseling process through reading, attending youth conventions, and taking counseling courses in a college or seminary. On the other hand, it is likely that most of the readers of this book are not interested in becoming full-time, professionally licensed therapists. The intent of this book is to hit the middle of these two positions. I hope that you will feel neither patronized nor intimidated.

The material is based on current theory and practice within the field of counseling. You will learn about the uniqueness of the counseling role, gain some tools for counseling teenagers, understand special requirements of counselors, know when to refer teenagers and/or their families to a professional counselor, and appreciate the need to take care of yourself. The material is practical, realistic, and useful. Many examples are used that will enable you to know exactly how to implement a particular counseling technique, design a counseling plan, and intervene in a crisis. Most youth workers will be able to say, "I can do that!"

The material in this book can be read by the individual youth worker, or it can serve as the basis for a counseling seminar or class for youth workers interested in improving their knowledge and expertise in counseling teenagers. Although not a "religious" book, the approach and foundation of the writer is Christian in perspective. Christian youth workers will find it complements their own faith, but it need not offend youth workers who serve teenagers in secular youth organizations.

In the end, the combination of your own personhood and the counseling skills you develop will enable you to uniquely assist those teenagers in your sphere of influence. Don't wait to counsel young people until you think you have everything mastered. You are likely to spend a lifetime learning the nuances of the counseling process. Get started, and you will gain experience and expertise.

I trust this book will be but one of the many helpful resources you have on your bookshelf. I wish you well as you help fragile teenagers become healthy, responsible, mature adults.

William J. Rowley
La Mesa, California

One

DEVELOPING RELATIONSHIPS WITH TEENAGERS

There is a long-standing assumption that teenagers don't listen to adults. On the surface, this seems to make sense. After all, teens are self-centered, socially oriented to other teenagers, and focused on their own agenda. But—*the assumption isn't true.* Evidence suggests that this commonly held view is nothing more than a myth.

In fact, the reverse may be more true. Adults tend not to listen to teenagers. Peter Buntman and E.M. Saris, in their book *How to Live with Your Teenager,* said, "Knowing how to listen is probably the most important communication tool there is. So few parents listen well."

Conjure up in your mind's eye a person, other than your parents, who made a significant impact on your life during your own teenage years. If you are like many of us, the image before you was that of an *adult,* not a teenager. Perhaps you thought of a sensitive teacher, an encouraging coach, a friendly neighbor, an affirming aunt or uncle, or a supportive member of your church.

As I think back to my own teen years, a kind and generous man comes to mind. He came into my life when I was about ten years old and remained there until I graduated from high school. Since my mother and father had divorced when I was ten months old, he was the first and most significant adult male in my life. Initially he was a friend of the family. Later, along with his wife, he became my youth leader at church. Finally he ended up being like a dad to me.

I had teenage friends in my life who were important to me. I usually had a best friend and a lot of acquaintances my own age. I dated and went steady during high school. I was involved in school activities. But I remember this adult man who dared to get involved in my life as being significant in helping me toward healthy adulthood.

As a counseling professional in private practice, I generally have several adolescents in my caseload. They are usually sent to my office by their parents. When I ask them why they have come, almost every one of them will say, "My parents sent me here." Now I must admit that many counseling professionals will tell you it is most difficult to get teenagers to shift from coming for counseling because they were sent, to coming because they want to work through a conflict. But this doesn't mean they refuse to listen.

Five years ago, for example, a mother sent her teenage daughter to see me. This young adolescent was in crisis. She was depressed, angry, and uncertain. It was a challenge to keep her in counseling for several months. But when she left my office for the last time, she had improved. The complete results, however, were far from clear. Recently I was able to get an update on this young woman when I unexpectedly saw her mother. "You'd be so proud of my daughter," she told me. "She graduated from high school on time, she is now attending college, and she wants to major in psychology!"

It appears that teenagers have a secret. They turn to other teenagers to find out how to be a teenager, and they listen to adults to learn what adulthood is all about. They just don't let us know this directly. We have to figure it out in retrospect.

The Making of a Myth
How did this myth that teenagers don't listen to adults get started? The answer can be found in developmental psychology. The psychological task of **adolescence** is the development of an organized, coherent, consistent sense of self. Erik Erikson was the first to elaborate extensively on this teenage task in his cornerstone work titled, *Identity: Youth and Crisis.*

Simply stated, it is the work of teenagers to develop an **identity** apart from their parents. Teens must be able to project themselves into the future with the confidence that they will be able to love and work as independent persons in their own right.

This task, however, is easier to describe than to accomplish. Parents are strong and influential, and can easily overwhelm a young person's first wobbly steps toward adulthood. Teens already know what their parents feel, think, and believe. In the presence of their parents, it is difficult for them to discern what is their own and what belongs to their parents. Therefore, they separate from their parents, literally creating physical and emotional distance so they can determine their own uniqueness and individuality — a process psychologists call **individuation.**

It is in this process that the seeds of the myth begin. Teens don't talk to their parents as much because parents have a tendency to teach and correct if what they hear and see isn't what they believe. Young people close the doors to their rooms in an attempt to experience themselves apart from other family members. They spend time away from home noting what it is like to make independent decisions and develop their own relationships. As their parents feel this distance, they double their efforts to guide their teens, and teens resist with direct and indirect messages that say, "Leave me alone. I know what *you* think. I need to learn what *I* think." Thus, the myth comes to fruition: Teens don't listen to adults.

Teenagers *do* listen to their parents; they just don't typically acknowledge this fact. And, more importantly for the youth leader, adolescents do listen to other adults who are not their parents. A daughter, for example, may need to separate herself from her parents, but a youth leader is not her parent. She can listen to her youth leader, knowing that he or she is more like a model adult, one she can emulate if she so chooses. This fact makes it possible for youth workers to impact young people in a positive, significant way. In fact, one of the wisest things Christian parents can do for their teens is to make sure there is a Christian youth worker in their lives. Youth leaders can become models and mentors to teens and allies of parents.

A Process, Not an Event

There would be little need for a youth leader if teens did not listen to significant adults. The fact that they do is the foundation on which the youth leader's relationship with adolescents rests. And, due to the fact that these young people are extremely social, there are many opportunities to interact with them in positive and constructive ways.

It can be reassuring to the adult working with teens to know that not every moment spent with these emerging adults has to be a significant turning point in their lives. Their fast-paced activity may suggest growth to be a continuous, high-intensity experience. As adults, however, we know that growth has peaks, valleys, and many more plateaus. The actual process of integrating various personality characteristics into a unified whole takes time.

Susan Littwin, in her book *The Postponed Generation,* suggests it is now taking today's young people up to ten extra years to complete the maturation process. We now have young people in their twenties who are still working on this important task. Many professionals in the mental health field believe this need for more time is due to the fact that today's world is so complex, technical, and specialized that both male and female adolescents are faced with thousands of choices and opportunities unknown and unavailable to previous generations.

In any case, adolescence is a process rather than an event. So there is time for what appears on the surface to be meaningless conversations with youth. There will also be occasions for the teachable moment, a time when the teenager is open to your wisdom and experience. Finally, there will be crisis moments and turning points, after which the adolescent can never quite be the same. All these experiences—some in which the youth leaders will be involved—eventually come together in such a way as to mold the unique individuality of each young person.

Rapping, Teaching, Preaching, and Advising

It is my experience that adults who relate well to teens are able to do so because they have a variety of interaction modes. Each mode is important, each can be more appropriate than the others depending on the purpose of the moment, and each can eventually serve as a bridge or door to use of the others. Knowing when and how to interact appropriately can increase the quality of a relationship with anyone, but especially with a teenager.

The first type of interaction is what a teen might call **rapping**. Teens do a lot of this, and they do it in conjunction with "hanging out." Rapping is a time when it appears to adults as though not much of importance is going on. It is as if no one is interested in much of anything, no one is in crisis, time is limitless, and there is no discernable direction. There are lots of grunts, laughs, and bravado. It is light conversation, what my generation might have called "chatting." To believe rapping is a waste of time, however, is to misunderstand the process and miss an opportunity to relate to teenagers.

The content may appear insignificant, but the process is extremely important to young people. Rapping allows for exploration, for sharing, for deciding, for trying, for comparing, for integrating, for listening, for accepting. It's a part of how teens "figure it all out" in a nonthreatening, unhurried atmosphere. No one makes a move until it is "safe" to do so. But the most important thing is that rapping provides kids with a mechanism for becoming emotionally connected to each other.

Adults who learn to rap can keep connected to their young people. These adults are more likely to know the concerns, the dreams, the fears, the hopes, and the problems their teens are facing. And, when at a later time teens are open to guidance or need counseling during a crisis, these adults are more likely to be involved in the process.

Rapping means that we adults must set aside our agendas, our schedules, our immediate goals, our need to lead. We must learn to slow down, relax, be there, hang out! The payoff can be immense. Rapping allows for emotional connecting and provides a later entrance to more meaningful moments of interaction with teenagers.

The second type of interaction with teens is that of **teaching.** At its core, teaching is giving something away to someone who wants or needs to know. It's as if you are saying, "This is what I have learned. It may be useful to you. If it is, great! If not, that's OK too."

Those of you who have worked with teenagers know that perhaps the worst scenario a teenager can conceive is being the only person who doesn't know the score. Teens will go to great lengths to hide their lack of knowledge or experience, even if it means bending the truth. About two weeks into my son's high school career, he proudly announced what he had learned. "I think I have high school figured out," he said. "You just act like you know what's going on!"

When you think about it, hundreds of experiences during junior and senior high school are "firsts." Everything from changing classrooms to having your own locker, to going to the mall without your parents, to driving, to dating, to taking the SAT or ACT, to applying for college admission is a first-time experience. And these are the easy problems to figure out!

Other adjustments are more complex. Like the young high schooler who accepts a new job but doesn't know about giving his previous employer "notice." He ends up with two jobs, not knowing what to do about it. Or the young man who finds himself going with two young ladies because he doesn't know how to break up with one of them. Or the students who find out they don't have enough money to pay for the burgers and fries they just ate. Or those who don't know what to do with their brand-new sexual feelings.

The disadvantage of parents, of course, is that their kids experience their teaching as "parental." "Mom, stop telling me what to do!" is a frequently heard response. Other significant adults, however, can teach the same lesson, share their wisdom and experience, and teens are more apt to listen. Perhaps because when I am teaching *your* kid, I don't have as much invested. I can handle your son or daughter saying to me, "Thanks, but I think I would rather do it another way." But when *my* kid says that too me, I think he is rebellious, unappreciative, or stupid! I end up feeling rejected.

I remember the adolescent whose mother was extremely upset

when she found a *Playboy* magazine in her son's room. It was an emotionally charged moment for her and an embarrassing one for him. For the youth leader, however, this would have been a great opportunity to teach on the topic of sexuality as it relates to the Christian life.

Can you hear yourself beginning the lesson? "Isn't it wonderful that your sexuality was created by God? He has, however, created a context in which the expression of your sexuality provides the most meaning and pleasure: marriage. You see, the problem with magazines is that they present women (or men) as sex objects rather than as individuals of value and worth who were created by God as sexual beings. That can get in the way as you try to relate to members of the opposite sex as whole people. Rather than relating to a person, you are responding only to a body. Such behavior is demeaning."

As a youth leader, you have completed a lesson on sexuality with a Christian perspective. Parents could do this as well. Most parents, however, would be too emotionally upset to realize the opportunity the magazine presents. As a dad or mom we are more likely to say, "Hey, what do you think you're doing? Looking at those pictures is wrong. Don't you ever let me catch you doing that again! Do you hear me?" It would be an opportunity missed.

Teaching is an objective, yet personal, tool that enables us to give what we have learned to teenagers in our charge. They may be grateful that we have kept them from looking foolish in front of their peers, and prevented them from making mistakes, some of which could have had lifelong consequences.

Another way to interact with teens is **preaching.** Few teenagers want to be "preached at." On the other hand, if preaching is letting young people know the truth, then it is an appropriate mode of interacting with them. In the end, teens may even thank us for proclaiming God's Word.

Many years ago, my wife and I were the youth leaders of a group of high school students in a small church we were attending. We had planned an evening to provide our teens with an opportunity to share their faith with their unchurched friends from school. We planned, prayed, and prepared for the event. There was to be entertainment and food—what we thought was a winning combination when it came to teenagers. On the night of the event, however, only our young people were in attendance. Not one visitor could be found.

Finally, one of our kids confronted this awkward situation directly. "No one is here but us," she said. I asked the group why this was so. This same teenager quietly said, "I didn't invite any of my friends. I wasn't sure I had anything to share." On one hand, such a remark could have been devastating. On the other hand, it presented us with a "preachable moment." Here was an opportunity to share God's

Word with our teens. All of us need God's redeeming grace, and when we receive it, we are to share with others what we have been given.

A few months ago, I received a phone call from a man. Over twenty years ago he had been one of the young people present on the night of that "sermon." Here is what he shared with me: "My older brother is teaching at a Christian college in the Boston area. My younger brother is teaching at a Christian college in the Northwest. I am a pastor of a church. I just wanted you to know that you guys meant a lot to me, and I thought you would want to know what happened to all of us."

As an adult who works with teenagers, can you imagine hearing anything that would surpass the joy of that conversation? Teens are interested in the truth. They can and do respond. We plant the seed as youth leaders, and God gives the increase.

A fourth interaction mode with teens is **advising.** The purpose of advising is to suggest alternative solutions. It's possible that you may give advice to a teen regarding a problem you haven't experienced. It's as though you are saying, "If that problem were mine, I think I might ... " Perhaps you could make two or three suggestions for handling the problem.

Let's suppose that one of the teens in your youth group is having difficulty with her father. The dialogue might go something like this:

"Does your father know you were hurt by what he said?"

"No, he wouldn't care anyway."

"Well, I think if it were my dad, I would find a way to talk to him about it. It's possible he doesn't know the impact he has on you."

"He wouldn't listen. He usually interrupts me before I can finish."

"Then you might try writing him a letter. End it by telling him you would like to talk about it after he finishes reading it."

Teens are by nature egocentric. It is difficult for them to see any viewpoint but their own. A sound piece of advice, without any pressure to act on it, can broaden their perspective on a subject and give them ideas for handling it, ways they hadn't thought of themselves. Sometimes our advising them can help them through difficult blocks in their relationships.

The Privilege of Counseling
A final way to relate to teenagers is **counseling,** the primary focus of this book. It is helpful to conceptualize counseling as "coming alongside another." The *process* of counseling is as important as the *product* (outcome). In our context, the youth worker and the teenager agree to work on a problem or conflict the teen is experiencing. It means that the teen has invited the youth worker to get involved. He will share his feelings, thoughts, and perceptions with you, and allow

you to work through the problem with him.

As you begin the counseling process, you may not have enough data to fully understand the problem or conflict. Therefore, you may have no idea initially what the solution will be.

It is even possible that, as the counselor, you may never have experienced the same problem the teenager is presenting. For example, perhaps you were pretty focused on your direction as a teenager, your parents' marriage was stable, and you experienced little confusion regarding your identity. Conversely, suppose the adolescent asking for your help was adopted as an infant. During this time of developing one's identity, this young person is experiencing difficulty knowing who he is. For the first time in his life, he recognizes that he has gaps in his past. He doesn't know who his biological parents are. He has a continuous stream of questions: "Why did my mother give me away?" "I wonder, do I look like my real parents?" "Didn't they love me?" Neither you nor the teenager knows the answers to these questions.

As a youth worker in a counseling mode, you have the privilege to "come alongside" this young, emerging adult. His questions are significant. As he resolves the conflicts within himself over his identity, you will have helped him toward healthy adulthood. This young person may be sharing with you the most painful part of his life to date, and his successful resolution may be among the most important endeavors of his entire life. And you will have been a part.

Rapping, teaching, preaching, and advising potentially lead to a counseling relationship with teenagers. In fact, few teens probably share with any adult vulnerable parts of themselves unless the adult has elicited their trust. This is usually done in the less threatening forms of interaction. The effective youth worker can and does relate to teens in all of these ways as situations warrant. When teenagers allow you the opportunity to enter a counseling relationship with them, when they invite you to help them, when they ask you to come alongside, it is the highest honor they can bestow on an adult.

Two

THE UNIQUE
PROCESS OF COUNSELING

Opportunities to counsel teenagers most often occur informally and spontaneously. Adults working with teens will therefore want to be alert to these opportunities whenever and wherever they happen. Unlike a mental health setting, where the young person enters into a formal, scheduled, narrowly defined counselor/client relationship, the adolescent in the real world sends out low-key signals that become an invitation for you to change to your counseling role.

Although it is possible for a teenager to be highly troubled, most counseling opportunities will center on issues of healthy growth and development. You may not be an expert in helping to lead a troubled teen out of severe depression or drug abuse—a situation which you most likely would refer to a psychotherapist—but you are likely to know quite a bit about adolescent development, and you have already been through the teen years yourself. You know something of the pitfalls and challenges of the teen years and can serve as a guide to the young people in your charge.

Several years ago, a young man was finishing his senior year in high school. He was intelligent, a member of the honor roll, and a leader in his church youth group. But like most teenagers, his friendships with peers were of utmost importance to him.

He had been planning to attend a church-related college in the fall, but had impulsively changed his mind. Instead, he had decided to delay going to school for a year so that he could go with a close friend of his, who was a junior in high school.

One day he stopped by the home of his youth leader, apparently just to rap. Embedded in his talk, however, he let it be known that he was delaying his decision to go to school. And then he paused, as if waiting for his youth leader to respond. The alert youth leader heard the signal. (A counseling moment can occur just that fast.) In this case, the young man quietly, unexpectedly was saying, "I've made a decision. I'm not sure about it. I'd like to know what you think." Notice the response the youth worker used:

Youth Worker: "Oh. The last I heard you were all set to go to school. What changed your mind?"

Teenager: "I think it would be fun to wait a year. Tom will graduate by then and we can room together."

Youth Worker: "Are you sure Tom is going?"

Teenager: "I haven't talked with him about it, but I think he would go if I waited a year and we went together."

Youth Worker: "It would be great for you guys to go together. You've always been great friends. But it doesn't sound like an absolutely sure thing that Tom is going. It would be a shame for you to delay your plans for a year only to find out he isn't going."

Teenager: "But, I don't know anybody else who's going."

Youth Worker: "It sounds like you're not feeling too sure about going to college by yourself."

Teenager: "Yeah! I'd like to go, but I'd rather go with someone I know. Then I can be sure I'll have at least one friend. What do you think I should do?"

Youth Worker: "Well, I can't make that decision for you. What I do know is that going to college for the first time is probably scary for everyone. It was for me."

Teenager: "Really?"

Youth Worker: "It sure was! What I know about you, however, is that you're a good student, and you make friends easily. In spite of your fears, I think you have all the tools to succeed. Besides, I know about that school, and they plan all kinds of activities so you can meet people."

Teenager: "I'm not even sure if Tom is going to graduate on time."

18

Youth Worker: "Whether you wait for him or not, I believe you're going to have a great time in college! It just might be wise if you were sure you aren't putting off college unnecessarily."

Teenager: "Thanks. I'm glad we talked."

This example can be helpful for a couple of reasons. First, it is a true story. It is typical of a normal adolescent making a significant decision about his future and wanting to share the process with an important adult in his life. Second, it shows us that a caring adult, alert to a counseling opportunity, can provide a teenager with an effective process for making the transition from childhood to adulthood.

On the surface, this interaction appears deceptively simple. At the same time, the teenager was concerned enough to share his insecurity and indecision with a trusted adult in his life. He decided after his talk with his youth leader to go to college as originally planned. His friend did follow him a year later, but soon dropped out of college. What was it about this youth worker's approach that helped this young man make what turned out to be a wise decision for him? Let's contrast this scenario with another example.

About a month ago an amused mother told me of an interaction she had had with her thirteen-year-old daughter one day. Her daughter had just come home from school, and apparently she had had a bad day.

Teenager: "Life is crummy. I have no friends; no one likes me. I'm really depressed."

To her mother's dismay, she carried on for several more minutes about how awful life was. The more she talked, the more her mother's concern and fear increased.

Mother: "Now, Judy. I'm sure you have a lot of friends. Just the other day, you had two of your girlfriends here after school. It just isn't true that you haven't any friends."

Teenager: "O, Mother. You don't understand. Life is terrible, and I don't have any friends!"

Mother: "Now, dear. I'm your friend. Don't you know that? You can always come to me to talk. We'll always be best friends."

Teenager: "O, Mother! You're overreacting! All seventh-grade girls are depressed!"

This mother suddenly realized that her daughter was blowing off steam. She wasn't asking for advice, she wasn't pathologically depressed, and she didn't need her mother as her best friend. She had had a bad day, but she also figured tomorrow would be a better day.

What's the difference between these two incidents? What makes the first one a counseling session and the other not? Let's take a look at the characteristics that enable counseling to occur.

Elements of the Counseling Process

● *First, the counselor approaches a counseling opportunity with objectivity.* To do so enables us to hear where the teenager is coming from *before* we have drawn any conclusions. Our objectivity says to the teenager, "I'm interested in what you think and feel about the matter. Go on, I'm listening."

Although the mother in the second scenario obviously had good intentions, she was emotionally involved to the degree that she misread the situation. Every mother naturally wants her children to feel good about themselves, to have friends and a sense of well-being. In fact, in this case, the girl's mother wanted this so badly that she tried to talk her daughter out of her feelings, and she attempted to solve a non-existent problem. Who among us parents hasn't done the same thing with our children?

The counselor's objectivity says to the young person that it is OK to explore all angles of an issue. No pre-judgment has been made. There isn't one answer that the counselor already knows. The two of you will pursue an answer together in the counseling process.

Remember that objectivity doesn't mean a lack of care. It rather means that I care enough about you to set aside momentarily what I might think about the matter so that *you* can decide, with my help, what is best for you.

● *Second, the counselor gathers relevant information before drawing any conclusions.* Proper diagnosis and treatment planning can only be effective if all the facts are known. Already having drawn conclusions about someone inevitably leads to missing a relevant piece of information.

Obviously, a professional psychotherapist will need a comprehensive history regarding a patient. But the concept and principle is valid regardless of the level of counseling or training of the counselor. In the case of the young man and his decision regarding college, there could have been a number of valid reasons for his delaying college entrance: lack of finances; a once-in-a-lifetime opportunity; poor health; lack of maturity; family circumstances. A wise counselor would not automatically assume that delaying college was an invalid decision. A wise counselor would say, "Tell me more about it."

The youth worker who automatically concludes that this young man has made a mistake might be embarrassed on finding out that one of his parents is in the middle of a health crisis. And, it would obviously turn a teenager off if the trusted adult in his life said, "What do you mean you're not going to college? That's the craziest idea I've ever heard from you!" That's not counseling!

Gathering the appropriate information relative to the teen's circumstances enables us to effectively respond and assist young people to resolve their problems. Additionally, Lewis Wolberg, in his *Hand-*

book of Short-Term Psychotherapy, suggests that proper information not only helps the counselor in the counseling process, but also helps the counselee to feel cared for.

• *Third, the counselor is enabled to counsel because the counselee permits it.* This isn't always true in the mental health setting, as some clients are sent for counseling by order of the courts. Teens, however, strongly resist an adult's help unless they ask for it.

Teenagers must be open to the counseling process. Otherwise, they resist and withdraw. When you consider the developmental process of teens, their natural resistance to the assistance of adults is understandable. They are attempting to separate from their parents and trying to see who they are and how well they can do apart from the significant adults in their lives. Teens are therefore very selective as to the adults they permit to get involved in their lives.

This isn't to say that counselors hold no power in the counseling relationship with adolescents. When any of us can enter into and influence another's life, we are in a very powerful position. That's why we must enter into any counseling relationship with care and responsibility. We do not, however, seek power as something to be grasped. It is given to us as long as we do not abuse it.

• *Fourth, the counseling process is always based on trust.* This principle is actually true for any relationship. It's the pivotal point in our relationship with God. "Trust in the Lord with all your heart and lean not on your understanding; in all your ways acknowledge Him, and He will make your paths straight" (Proverbs 3:5-6).

Even though there are various strategies and techniques in counseling, the process begins when the counselee trusts the counselor enough to risk sharing his or her vulnerabilities. Counseling is more than a body of knowledge and a set of skills. It is first and foremost a relationship between people, based on their abilities to trust one another.

Teenagers will base this trust on the belief that you are interested in their welfare, that you will hold what is said in confidence, and that you will relate to them in an authentic manner.

• *Fifth, the counseling relationship is characterized by mutual respect.* Teenagers are emerging adults. They are in process, but they haven't reached their goal. Their egos, their sense of self, are fragile. The likelihood that they will share their vulnerabilities with an adult who acts superior, patronizes them, or talks down to them is close to zero. They need to know that they are safe with you.

Notice in the first scenario how the youth leader approached the young man in her youth group. She took what he said seriously. She mirrored the fact that this teen's concern regarding his decision was important to him. She stopped whatever else she might have been doing and gave his concern first priority. She was careful of the young man's insecurities and probably helped to strengthen his feelings of value and self-worth.

If the counselor doesn't respect the teenager, the counseling process is impaired. It is just as important, however, that the teenager respect the counselor. Teenagers simply won't listen to people whom they disrespect. In order for a counselor to influence or impact the attitudes, decisions, and behavior of teenagers, the teenagers must experience the counselor as an adult "worthy of respect."

• *Sixth, good counseling begins with good listening.* As stated earlier, most teens doubt that adults really listen to them. So when adults *do* listen, adolescents take notice. Good listening enables us to hear the words of a counselee, and interpret their meaning. It also gives the teenager the impression that you are really interested in him or her.

Most teenagers will begin a counseling opportunity with what mental health professionals call a **presenting problem.** Sometimes this problem isn't the counselee's real problem. Depending on how sensitively you handle this less anxiety-provoking concern, the teen will either move closer to or shy away from the real problem. Telling you of his decision to delay going to college for a year is less vulnerable than telling you that he is afraid to go away to college by himself. This process of a counselee beginning at one point and moving closer to the real issue means that it is imperative that the counselor *continuously* listen throughout the entire session.

The result of good listening pays dividends. Eventually, the teenager will throw you a clue as to the real concern. For example, the young man delaying his college entrance said, "I think it would be fun to wait a year. Tom will graduate by then and we can room together." The youth leader, wearing his or her counseling hat, will now have a pretty good idea what the problem is and can approach the problem with sensitivity. Eventually, the counselor in our example sensitively put this young man's fear into words. "It sounds like you're not feeling too sure about going to college by yourself."

Your patience and correct interpretation has paid off when your teenager concurs, as the young man in our example did. "Yeah! I'd like to go, but I'd rather go with someone I know. Then I can be sure I'll have at least one friend."

Assuming too quickly that you know what the problem is can result in your missing what the teenager is saying. A teenager generally notes this problem by saying, "You don't understand."

Several years ago, Carl Rogers, one of the most influential psychologists in the field of counseling, spoke to counseling professionals at a convention in San Diego. He defined counseling in a unique manner. He said it is something like a man buried in a cave, all alone, with the hope that someone will come along and help him out of the cave. In his hand is an object that he taps against the wall, hoping that someone will hear his faint signals. Day after day he beats out his signal for help, but no one hears him.

One day another person hears the man tapping his message. She taps out a response. The man in the cave is overjoyed and says to himself, "Finally, someone has heard me!" The counselor then goes to work, helping the man come out of his cave.

This is the way it is with teenagers. Much of what they are doing is for the first time. New experiences can be challenging, overwhelming, frightening. Just like adults, however, they grow skilled at hiding these vulnerable feelings from others. They can feel as though they are "buried" by their fears, insecurities, confusion. They quietly, faintly, carefully tap out their message to caring adults. If we are listening, we will hear their cry for help.

● *Seventh, the counselor and the counselee have different but complimentary roles.* The counselor listens, questions, mirrors, interprets, responds, affirms, encourages, supports. The responsibility of the counselor is to provide the process which enables the counselee to look at the issues and concerns of life, and to possibly make decisions that facilitate healthy growth and development. The adult counselor is not responsible for making decisions for teenagers. As a result of the counseling process, however, the teenager's decisions can be wiser ones. Although teens may not necessarily make wiser decisions, the counselor has fulfilled his or her responsibility by helping the teenager explore all facets of an issue before a decision is made.

It is the responsibility of teenagers to participate openly in the counseling process, and to make the decisions or changes in behavior that seem appropriate for the situation. Notice that the youth leader in the first scenario did not tell the young man what to do regarding college. She left the responsibility of that decision to him. What she did was to help him understand his feelings and the basis for his delaying college. She also gave him her perspective regarding his ability to make new friends, and she let him know of her faith in his judgment to make a decision that was best for him. It is not surprising, then, that this young man thanked her for her help.

● *Eighth, the nature of the counseling relationship is that of an alliance.* This type of relationship suggests that the counselor/counselee work together toward the teenager's good. Make no mistake about it. It is the teenager's journey; but the counselor journeys alongside. Professional counselors call this relationship a **therapeutic alliance.**

The agenda of counseling centers on the teenager's issues and concerns, and the counselor agrees to assist in the process as long as he or she believes it to be in the best interest and welfare of the young person and does not violate the counselor's own principles. Certainly a solid decision regarding college is in the best interest of a late adolescent. The counselor can enter into this agenda readily.

On the other hand, suppose a young adolescent girl in your youth group tells you she is using drugs and wants your help. She also wants you to promise that you will not tell anyone about her involvement in the drug scene. Remember that the counseling relationship is to be a *therapeutic* alliance. You therefore have the right and responsibility to determine whether a relationship is in the best interest of the counselee. If it isn't, you must refuse to participate in a process that may harm or injure the counselee.

In this instance, a young minor is asking you to promise something that is not in her best interest and hinders your ability to help her. You may (and should) decline to make such a promise. This doesn't mean you would abandon this young lady when she is asking for your help. Instead, you would try to get her to agree to an alliance that allows you to provide her with the kind of assistance she needs.

An example of such restructuring of your agreement might be as follows: "Mary, I'm really pleased you trusted me enough to ask for my help. I want to help you, but I cannot promise that I will tell no one of your drug involvement. That would make it impossible for me to help you. You need to trust that I will tell no one unless, in my judgment, they need to know in order for you to get the kind of help you need. For example, we need your parents' help. They will be initially upset, but I know they love you and will want to help any way they can. I will be there when you tell them, if it would help."

Fortunately, most of the issues and concerns brought to you by young people will be those in which you can participate without hesitation. Opportunities to work therapeutically with teenagers are many.

The Secret of Counseling

What is it about the counseling process that facilitates healthy growth and development? Certainly any one of the previously mentioned elements might be found in other modes of interaction between people. If there is any mystery to counseling, it is this: All these components, working together, encourage and enable the counselee to explain to another person what is inside him or her, and, when seen in the light of reality and the counselor's perspective, lead to improved clarity upon which new understanding, direction, and decision can be based. Put more simply, trying to make yourself understood by another person brings about better understanding of yourself. The resulting clarity becomes the basis for change, growth, and development.

The potential impact of an adult who counsels teenagers is incredible! Teenagers are evolving from childhood to adulthood. It is in this transition phase that the counselor provides the necessary ingredients for helping them inch toward maturity.

Three

QUALITIES OF
THE EFFECTIVE HELPER

A few years ago, I met a friend of mine for lunch at his office. He was a stockbroker and was talking to one of his clients on the phone when I arrived. I couldn't help but overhear his conversation as I waited for him. Naturally, I thought he would be providing financial advice regarding an up-and-coming stock. But such was not the case.

Instead, it became obvious that his client was talking to him about a personal problem. Here was a man with an MBA, working with high-powered businessmen wanting to make money. Something about my friend, however, elicited trust from these hard drivers, and they began to share their doubts and vulnerabilities with him.

As I watched and listened to my friend respond to his client in need, I was reminded of a fact that most of us know. *People gravitate toward certain people for help.* Lifelong helpers can usually tell you that their unique role began somewhat spontaneously early in their lives, perhaps in junior or senior high school. Perhaps you remember a student when you attended high school who served as the "counselor" for everyone. Kids talk to these young helpers about their problems with the opposite sex, parents, teachers, and anything else that concerns them.

Several years ago, I noticed that my teenage son had three female friends in his life. Although he was not really romantically involved with any of them, they apparently were important to him. One day I asked him what he saw in each of these girls that made them attractive to him. I was interested to hear him describe one of them by saying, "You can talk to her about anything."

All of this is intriguing because people talk to these helpers in spite of the fact that the helpers may have little or no formal training or experience as counselors. In the 1960s and 1970s, a significant amount of research was done to determine the reasons for this phenomenon. It was found that there are common characteristics or qualities held by these helpers. Your own efforts to help teenagers, regardless of your training or experience level, can be improved with the knowledge and practice of these key elements.

As a professional psychotherapist, I am not negating or in any way diminishing the value of education, training, or experience. Current research in applied psychology, for example, has documented the fact that there are specific therapy modalities used by the trained psychotherapist that prove more effective in the treatment of thought and mood disorders. I would recommend that as an adult who counsels youth, you gain as much knowledge and experience as you can. After all, it has been found that effective helpers generally have a thorough knowledge of their subject. But lay counselors can be *more effective* as they display these qualities, and the trained professional can be *less effective* without them.

During my own training, I remember reading the Combs, Avila, and Purkey study titled *Helping Relationships: Basic Concepts for the Helping Professions.* I was particularly impressed with their research that suggested that the effectiveness of a helper was "a question of the use of the helper's self, the peculiar way in which he (she) is able to combine his (her) knowledge and understanding with his (her) unique ways of putting it into operation to be helpful to others."

This is an exciting concept for any adult who has made a commitment to work with teenagers. It means that each of us brings to the task of counseling a unique self, that, when combined with elements that prove helpful, can greatly assist young people in their growth and development.

Characteristics of the Effective Helper

In the *Florida Studies in the Helping Professions,* Combs and others found that effective counselors, among other helping professionals, had "a high degree of similarity" in the perceptions they held regarding themselves, other people, the problems they faced, and the manner in which they proceeded to help others. It should prove helpful to look at each of these elements in light of the counseling process.

● *First, effective helpers perceive themselves as adequate, trustworthy, wanted, and worthy.* This is not to suggest that they have a distorted, exaggerated, arrogant view of themselves. Rather, they present a quiet acceptance of their own personhood. They are aware of both their strengths and weaknesses. They have a clear idea, therefore, of what they have to offer others. On the other hand, they have no need to be who they are not, and they recognize their limitations. They are comfortable with themselves and are not surprised that you might want to talk to them.

The fact that effective helpers tend to have a positive view about themselves has an air of credibility about it. We are drawn to people who know and are accepting of themselves. Scott Peck, in his book *The Road Less Traveled,* suggests that it is only as we recognize and accept who we are that we can face the areas of our lives in which we need to grow and mature. Until we get to this point, we spend our energy denying and hiding our vulnerabilities from others. There is little energy left to risk growth.

Helpers appreciate their own value and can therefore face their own struggles courageously. They serve as an inspiration for others to do the same. Due to their balanced, healthy view of themselves, we experience them as soft, gentle, and helpful. After all, if they are patient and accepting of themselves, they seem more likely to treat us the same way.

Can you imagine a teen working with a leader who does not have a healthy self-image? Consider the "helpfulness" of this dialogue:

Teenager: "Sometimes I don't think anyone likes me."

Youth Leader: "This sounds serious. I don't know what to say. I'm sure that someone else could be more helpful than I can."

Teenager: "But I wanted to talk to you. Did you ever feel like this when you were in high school?"

Youth Leader: "Look, I don't know why you would want to talk to me about this. I'm just not the one to help you. Why don't you talk to Mary? She'd be great!"

Teenager: "Oh. OK."

This illustration is exaggerated, but would you be drawn to a counselor who gave you the impression that your concerns as a teenager cause him discomfort and feelings of inadequacy? Such a counselor would cause my anxiety to increase if I were that young person. Notice that this teenager was not asking for an immediate solution to his perceived problem. He just wanted to talk about his feelings, and he wondered if his youth leader had experienced similar feelings during his own teenage years.

Contrast that dialogue with a conversation I had with an adult layperson who attends a large, attractive church in my community:

> **Karen:** "There's this young lady at my church who is a friend of my daughter. She seems to talk to me about everything."
>
> **Bill:** "That's a real compliment. Do you feel OK about her wanting to talk to you?"
>
> **Karen:** "Oh, sure. I told her that I don't have the answers to everything, but I really appreciate her trust in me. I told her to feel free to talk to me anytime she wanted to."

I knew immediately that this adult had a quiet confidence about herself that drew this young teenager to her.

All of us feel inadequate at times, but effective helpers seem to know intuitively that each of us has something unique that is just what someone else needs. They are comfortable with the fact that someone else has chosen them, trusts them, and wants to be helped by them.

Several years ago, Sydney Jourard wrote *The Transparent Self* for counseling professionals. The premise of the book was simple but profound: Transparency begets transparency. I have found in my own counseling practice and personal experience that a sense of self-acceptance and a sense of self-regard are enablers in helping people open themselves up to another.

Everett Shostrom defines both self-acceptance and self-regard in the *Manual for the Personal Orientation Inventory*. He describes self-acceptance as "affirmation or acceptance of self in spite of weaknesses or deficiencies." Self-regard, on the other hand, is seen by Shostrom as "affirmation of self because of worth and strength." Shostrom suggests that the healthy person has a high degree of both self-acceptance and self-regard.

Even Scripture suggests the need for this balanced view of self. Romans 5:8 clearly tells us of God's value of us in the midst of our shortcomings. "But God demonstrates His own love for us in this: While we were still sinners, Christ died for us." God values us, and so do others. Effective helpers know this and are comfortable with it.

● *Second, effective helpers have a high degree of confidence in other people.* This seems to serve as a counterbalance with their positive feelings about themselves. The *Florida Studies* found that helpful individuals see others as friendly, well-intentioned, worthy, as having dignity and integrity, as being trustworthy, dependable, predictable, and as being potentially fulfilling and enhancing to self.

In our day, it is easy to be discouraged, frustrated, and disappointed in the shortcomings of others. The more one sees of this world, the more one is tempted to become cynical, to see others as self-centered, self-indulgent, and manipulative. A.L. Williams, in his book *All You Can Do Is All You Can Do But All You Can Do Is Enough* writes about this theme. "Most people have been so hurt and so disappointed by other people that they just can't believe that human beings have the potential to be good."

Williams continues, "Other people are pretty much like you. . . . They've been hurt, too, and as much as you'd like to think they can tell you're different, they are just as hesitant to trust as you are." Effective helpers, however, seem to be able to rise above all of this. It isn't that they are naive of the suffering around them. They seem to have faith that each of us desires to rise above our pain, and that we can do so if given help.

The perceptions of effective helpers regarding themselves and others reminds me of the concept of "basic life positions" as described by Transactional Analysis (TA) proponents. According to TA, a school of psychology, the four basic life positions are as follows: (1) "I'm OK — You're OK"; (2) "I'm OK — You're Not OK"; (3) "I'm Not OK — You're OK"; and (4) "I'm Not OK — You're Not OK."

Some Christians have felt threatened by the concept of "I'm OK — You're OK." They have therefore come up with another life position: "I'm not OK, and you're not OK, but Christ makes us both OK." Perhaps these Christians have interpreted the "I'm OK — You're OK" life position as denying our basic sinfulness and need of Christ in our lives. Such an interpretation of this life position, however, was never meant by TA followers.

Each of the basic life positions was meant to be a description of the *perceptions* we have about ourselves and others. They are not declarations of *fact*. The point being made is that effective helpers hold the position of "I'm OK — You're OK." It's the position that says, "This is who we are. It's a given that we have strengths and weaknesses. Now that that's out of the way, we can get to work on the areas that need growth, and we will do so in an accepting, affirming, hopeful atmosphere."

According to Gerald Corey's *Theory and Practice of Counseling and Psychotherapy,* the other three life positions involve either the projecting of blame for one's problems on others, the distancing and withdrawing from others because we feel powerless and inferior to others, or the giving up all hope because life has no promise.

Effective helpers resist these life positions. They believe in others and place themselves in the position of offering any assistance they can to help those who are confused, discouraged, and troubled. They confidentially believe that people can grow, improve, and mature.

• *Third, effective helpers identify with, get involved with, and have a genuine interest in people.* In fact, they are more interested in people than they are in things. They do not approach others in a detached, aloof, distant manner. They feel connected and consider themselves a part of the human condition.

29

Effective counselors make themselves emotionally and physically available to others. Such behavior was, of course, modeled by Jesus. "Your attitude should be the same as that of Christ Jesus: Who, being in very nature God, did not consider equality with God something to be grasped, but made Himself nothing, taking the very nature of a servant, being made in human likeness" (Philippians 2:5-7).

Jesus was involved, available, and connected to others. He did not remain detached, aloof, or distant. He became one of us, identified with our suffering, and therefore can effectively help us.

As I listen to clients in my office, I have often thought, *I have had this problem, I have resolved a similar problem, or I could experience this problem in the future!* If you are "there" with others, it is difficult to remain aloof and detached.

Perhaps you can identify with our earlier example of the teenager who felt no one liked him. As a youth worker, it is often difficult to nurture and maintain friendships with adults your own age due to the fact that you are with teenagers all the time. Perhaps we can change the dialogue with this teenager in such a way that we identify with him and help him explore his feelings.

Teenager: "Sometimes I don't think anyone likes me."

Youth Leader: "Tom, I'm not aware of that, but what makes you think so?"

Teenager: "Oh, I don't know. It just looks like everybody else has all kinds of friends. Did you ever feel like this when you were in high school?"

Youth Leader: "I sure did. In fact, sometimes I feel that way now."

Teenager: "You do? Wow! Everybody likes you. How could you feel this way?"

Youth Leader: "Well, I have found my feelings are not always the facts. But, I feel this way anyway when I am really busy or my schedule doesn't allow me to be with my friends."

Teenager: "What do you do?"

Youth Leader: "I try to look at what's really true. I begin to realize that it isn't that no one likes me; I'm just too busy, and I need to make contact with my friends."

Teenager: "Maybe I need to call Johnny."

Adults who work with teenagers identify with and are very involved with others. It's impossible to lead young people or counsel them unless you "get in there with them."

• *Fourth, effective helpers have a unique perception of how to approach the task of helping others.* They tend to be:

    —freeing rather than controlling;

    —concerned with larger issues rather than smaller ones;

    —self-revealing rather than self-concealing;

—process-oriented rather than goal-oriented;

—oriented to the needs of others rather than their own.

It isn't difficult to see that authentic growth is better facilitated by creating an atmosphere that allows teenagers to explore fully their feelings, attitudes, values, personality, behavior, strengths, weaknesses, goals, dreams, faith, and fears. A controlling relationship may lead to a teenager doing what *we* want, but this may not be an expression of growth or authentic expression of self. Such a young person may be repressing who he or she really is or hindering the development of self in order to gain the approval of a significant other.

Such behavior is neither authentic nor congruent with the teen's inside self. Remember that the effective helper has confidence and trust in the young person's desire and ability to deal with his or her problems and to mature in a healthy manner if only encouraged to do so. Controlling one's growth may not be growth at all.

Counselors who provide a helpful relationship have an uncanny ability to sift and sort through all the information concerning another person and see the significant issues. In the earlier example of the teenager who was thinking of delaying the decision to go to college, the youth worker recognized the larger issue: the adolescent's insecurity about making new friends in a new setting.

Effective helpers, in other words, see the big picture. An adopted teen searching for her biological parents, for example, is dealing with the larger issue of identity. A young person who is experiencing conflict with his parents because they want him to be involved in all family activities is dealing with the need for separation. The teen who is in constant conflict with the rules at school may be struggling with her relationship with authority figures. The late adolescent who is afraid to leave home could be experiencing conflict between the need for independence and the need for dependence. The junior high school student who is acting up in order to impress others may be trying to bolster weak self-esteem.

Regardless of the specifics, helpful individuals are able to see the larger issue. They are not lost or distracted by irrelevant details. They see how smaller issues relate to larger ones. They seem to sense what needs to be dealt with immediately, what can be postponed, and what will probably work itself out spontaneously over time. They can discern a **crisis** from an **age-appropriate** problem, an issue that is normal for a specific age-span. A teenager who wants to close her door, decorate her room with posters, and clutter the furniture and floor with clothes and therefore comes into conflict with her compulsive, orderly parents is experiencing an age-appropriate problem rather than an emotional disorder. Effective helpers are characterized by their ability to make these distinctions.

Helpful individuals are not afraid of sharing themselves with those with whom they interact. They are self-revealing. Laymen call this characteristic openness or transparency. Mental health professionals call it **self-disclosure.**

For many of us, self-disclosure suggests that we share incidents, experiences, moments in our life that were meaningful to us. It is a kind of historical sharing of our lives with others. Such self-disclosure of ourselves in a counseling session may or may not be helpful. This kind of sharing is focused on ourselves rather than the other person, and is a recollection of the past.

Effective helpers self-disclose in a significantly different manner. They share their current responses to what is going on as a result of interacting with another. For example, let's say you notice that a young man in your youth group is continually self-deprecating when he is a part of the larger group. When you are with him one-on-one, however, there is a noticeable absence of this behavior. A comment that discloses your current response to his behavior might sound like this: "Fred, I feel frustrated when I hear you put yourself down all the time. It seems to me that you really batter yourself in our group. You don't do it when you're just with me. I'm wondering why you feel the need to put yourself down with your friends."

Such a comment reveals your inner response to his behavior. It brings to the surface in a transparent, caring way your observation and response to this teen's behavior. Such self-disclosure is in the here-and-now rather than past history, and it centers not on self but on the other person. Since your response is happening *now*, it doesn't sound like a lecture you have been waiting to deliver. The comment isn't judgmental. Essentially, you are telling this young man that you feel frustrated when he treats himself in a way that you feel he doesn't deserve.

In counseling sessions, such self-disclosure encourages the counselee to confront the observed behavior in a nonjudgmental atmosphere. It facilitates exploration and understanding on the part of the other person in the relationship.

Effective helpers also recognize that *how one reaches the goal* is as important as the goal itself. Louis L'amour, the western writer, stated it in a unique way in his book *Ride the Dark Trail.* "The thing to remember when traveling is that the trail is the thing, not the end of the trail. Travel too fast, and you'll forget what you're traveling for."

Wise counselors often recognize "the answer" before a client does as they explore an issue together. The counselors recognize, however, that to "give" the answer prematurely or to prevent the counselee from processing the answer for himself often takes away the power of discovery. The counselor's answer just doesn't seem to have the significant impact of an answer arrived at by the counselee.

The counselee may reach the end of the trail, but an important part of the journey is the trail itself. After all, the teenager with whom you are counseling needs to feel good about what *he* discovered.

There is a whole different feeling to being thanked for your wisdom than there is when a counselee says to you, "Wow! I think I understand what's going on. I've never seen it before!" The effective helper knows that a good process generally brings a good result. One need not worry so much about the goal or the outcome as long as careful planning and work take place.

Several years ago, a father and his teenage son decided to see the Boston Red Sox play a game in Fenway Park. I suppose this activity (goal) was in itself of value and worth since it is always beneficial to nurture a father/son relationship. What made this trip unique, however, was that these two people lived in California!

Soon, the process of getting to Boston took precedence over the game itself. They decided to go by train, which would take two and a half days and three nights. Mile after mile they talked, read, ate, wrote, and looked at the country passing outside the train window. The train was late, they missed a connection in Chicago, they took an alternate train to Philadelphia, and finally decided to fly to Boston from Philadelphia in order to reach the game on time.

Fenway Park is filled with tradition. They had great seats behind home plate. The Red Sox won the game over Kansas City by one run in the ninth inning in a come-from-behind victory. It was a great game. But what they remember in vivid detail, what they talk and laugh about, what only the two of them experienced, is not the game. They remember the trip to the game.

It was a hard trip, a long trip, a grinding trip. They had traveled from coast to coast to make the game. The young man put into words what helpers seem to know. Just before the game started, he said, "Dad, it doesn't matter whether Boston wins or not. The important thing is that we got here."

Effective helpers recognize the value of the process. They are process-oriented rather than goal-oriented. They want to reach their goal, and they often do, but they also wait to make sure the goal is reached carefully and wisely. When you're traveling, the trail's the thing.

Finally, helpers are typically more tuned into the needs of others than they are to their own needs. They hear others' needs, they anticipate others' needs, they make others' needs a priority, sometimes sacrificing their own needs.

Personal Characteristics That Facilitate Healthy Change

We have been describing common perceptions held by effective helpers regarding themselves, others, and the task of helping others.

Knowing these characteristics can give insight about what is and what isn't helpful in working with adolescents. It is possible to pare the list down to three qualities that can serve as the central part of any therapeutic relationship with a teenager: **congruence, unconditional positive regard,** and **accurate empathic understanding.**

Research suggests that these three personal characteristics or attitudes form the core of the counseling relationship. Carl Rogers, in his classic book *On Becoming a Person,* said, "If I can provide a certain type of relationship, the other person will discover within himself the capacity to use that relationship for growth and change, and personal development will occur." Rogers, an expert in the field of psychology and counseling, was talking about a relationship characterized by a counselor who demonstrates these three qualities.

The first quality, congruence, is sometimes called genuineness. Its essence is that the effective counselor is "real." According to Corey's book, *Theory and Practice of Counseling and Psychotherapy,* "The therapist is genuine, integrated, and authentic. . . ." It seems almost unnecessary to suggest that counselors need to be real! And yet, it is easy to get lost in what we think we should say or do in order to help someone else.

What is helpful, however, is to express to a counselee what is being experienced by you on the inside when the situation warrants it. This suggests a spontaneity, an openness that actually serves to disarm the person being helped. In other words, it is therapeutic to share the feelings and attitudes, positive as well as negative, you are experiencing as a result of the interaction going on at the moment.

For example, suppose you are talking to a teenager who has very few friends in your youth group. As you talk to him, he is arrogant, feels superior to the other kids, puts them down, and is generally negative about everyone. A congruent response from you might be: "You know, Harry, I experience you as somewhat intimidating. You are so negative, so judgmental about everyone around you. I have begun to wonder if you feel the same way about me."

As a youth leader, you may think that such a response might jeopardize your relationship with this young man. As amazing as it may seem, however, such an authentic, genuine response can serve to facilitate growth in Harry. His knowing how *you* feel as a result of his attitudes and behavior may serve to help him understand why he feels alienated from those around him.

Congruence means that you share outwardly what you are feeling or thinking inwardly. It is honest feedback that this young man may not have heard from others. Several years ago, I was talking to my teenage son. He was talking about a female friend of his who he described as "always up." He said it was difficult to relate to her very long because, "No one is *always* up." When I asked him if it might be helpful to tell her how he felt, he said, "No, I wouldn't want to hurt her feelings." I appreciated his sensitivity; but the girl never knew his real feelings either. I wondered how many others felt that way about her.

Naturally, there will be other times when your spontaneous remarks will be positive. Your responses, whether positive or negative, encourage free and open communication due to their authenticity and genuineness. Both people in the relationship are saying, "We're being real here." Rogers believed that congruency is the most important personal characteristic of the three attitudes that form the core of therapeutic relationships.

The second characteristic which contributes to a therapeutic relationship, unconditional positive regard, is sometimes called nonpossessive warmth. In a way, this quality is extremely Christlike because its essence is a deep, genuine caring for *who the person is.*

It is easy to get caught up in what people do rather than who they are or who they are becoming. Teenagers can be self-centered, inconsistent, insensitive, and obnoxious! An attitude of unconditional positive regard, however, means that our caring is not contingent on the adolescent's behavior. We do not withhold our caring until our judgment or evaluation of the teen's thoughts, feelings, or behavior is positive. As Corey says, "It is not an attitude of 'I'll accept you when'; rather it is one of 'I'll accept you as you are.' "

It needs to be made clear that we may not *approve* of a teenager's behavior. Our caring, however, is not withheld. Christ modeled this attitude in that He loves the sinner but disapproves of sin. He continuously cares for us.

Unconditional positive regard, our continuous caring, implies that we are nonjudgmental and nonpossessive regarding the individual's person. Due to our attitude, the teenager is more likely to evaluate his own behavior, thoughts, and feelings and decide the appropriateness of them. Because we accept teenagers as they are, they need not defend their actions and are more likely to modify dysfunctional behavior.

The last of the three characteristics that form the central core of a helpful relationship is accurate empathic understanding. Naturally it isn't possible for a counselor to have experienced everything a counselee has experienced. And, it is impossible to know exactly what another feels. The task nevertheless is to be able to understand as accurately as possible the subjective experience of the teenager you counsel.

As counselors listen, they try to sense what the counselee is feeling, even though these feelings are not their own. By trying to enter the world of teens, they become better able to help adolescents explore, understand, and perhaps change their behavior.

To illustrate this characteristic, imagine you are talking to one of the high school girls in your youth group. She missed her curfew and has been grounded for the next weekend. In addition to her grounding, however, her father has taken the door to her bedroom off its hinges, making it impossible for her to close off her room from the rest of the family. You know the family, and this young woman has two adolescent brothers.

Teenager: "My parents are just awful. They're so unfair!"

Youth Worker: "What happened?"

Teenager: "I missed my curfew, and they have grounded me for next weekend. I hate them!"

Youth Worker: "Why does that seem unfair to you? That seems to be a fairly common consequence when kids miss their curfew. You seem really mad."

Teenager: "They don't understand me! I don't know if I'll ever forgive them, particularly my brothers."

Youth Worker: "Estelle, what's going on? How do your brothers figure in the picture?"

Teenager: "They keep walking past my door when I'm dressing."

Youth Worker: "Why don't you just close your door?"

Teenager: "Because my Dad took the door off because I missed my curfew! My brothers keep walking past my door. They're jerks!"

Youth Worker: "Now I see why you said your family doesn't understand you. It must be terrible not having a door to your room."

Teenager: "It's awful. I feel like going to bed with my clothes on. I feel so . . . Oh, I don't know how I feel!"

Youth Worker: "You feel exposed. Like everyone is looking at you. Like there is no place you can go to have privacy."

Teenager: "Yes! Everybody is looking at me. I feel so embarrassed!"

The first clue to accurate empathic understanding was the intensity of this young girl's response to the fact that her parents grounded her for missing curfew. As you tried to get into her world, you recognized that her response was a bit overreactive to the grounding her parents gave her. When she was pressed about her response, she gave more information: "They don't understand me." Remembering your own teenage days, you probably would have said something similar if your parents' behavior failed to take into account something that was very important to you. Her next clue centered on her brothers, and the fact that she didn't think she could ever forgive them told you that you were dealing with something very important to this young girl.

By this time, you know that the problem is not an adolescent being grounded. So you ask her what is going on. Finally her concern is expressed: "My Dad took the door off my room." Can you imagine what it must feel like to be an emerging woman, having to dress in a room without a door, knowing that your teenage brothers are watching, and your parents appear oblivious to the embarrassment you feel?

Now you have about as accurate a "feel" for this young girl's subjective experience as you can get. You put it into words: "You feel exposed. Like everyone is looking at you." Notice that these words form a statement, not a question. A question would suggest that *you* don't understand this girl's plight either. But a statement, an accurate empathic statement, lets her know that you understand her.

In summary, congruence, unconditional positive regard, and accurate empathic understanding form the core of a therapeutic relationship. None of us is absolutely perfect in the expression of these characteristics or attitudes. Knowing how important they are, continually developing our expertise in their expression, and integrating them into our own personality will assist us greatly in providing teenagers with a therapeutic relationship in which to grow and mature.

Our Unique Personhood

As you review the characteristics and attitudes of effective helpers described in this chapter, you may become anxious and discouraged with your ability to counsel teenagers. Don't be. RELAX! Remember that the most important element you bring to a counseling relationship is *yourself.*

It is the hope of counselor educators who train counselors in colleges and universities that one's training, experience, knowledge, and intuition will become fully integrated into the personhood of the therapist. As a youth pastor, youth worker, or lay leader, this is your goal. You need not be perfect or all-knowing. Developing and integrating the characteristics described in this chapter can increase your effectiveness as a counselor. What makes these characteristics particularly effective, however, is the manner in which they interact with your unique personality.

Four

UNDERSTANDING
TODAY'S TEENAGER

Most of us try to understand teenagers through our own experience
as an adolescent. The concept seems simple and credible. "I was a
teenager once; therefore, I know what it's like for you to be a teenager." Chances are, however, that this is far from true. And, if you
continue to believe it, you may be out-of-step with today's teen.

To be sure, the general developmental process toward maturity is
similar to the journey previous generations traveled. Separation issues, the development of identity, the need to conform to adolescent
norms, the need to experience decision-making apart from parents,
for example, continue to be an integral part of the path today's young
people take.

What is the difference, then, between today's teens and those of
the past? The answer lies not so much in teenagers but in the world
in which they live. To be an effective counselor of these emerging
adults, we absolutely must recognize a profound and significant fact:
Today's teenagers are growing up in a vastly different world than the

one we adults experienced as teens. In many ways, we do not know what it is like to be a teenager today. We know, instead, what it was like to be a teenager in another world!

A couple of years ago I listened to the academic dean of a small, liberal arts, Christian college in my community. He was speaking to the parents of an incoming group of freshmen students. He was trying to describe to these parents the value of a liberal arts education, one that prepares a student to be generally aware of the core understandings of all the major disciplines of study. He told these parents, "We want our students to be broadly educated, with the ability to think and problem-solve, and to move in any number of directions as the world around them changes."

It was then that this educator made a statement that astounded his audience. "The latest studies suggest that your freshmen students, before they retire, will have made from four to five major career moves, and many of those moves will be to jobs that have not yet come into being." We have reached a point in our society in which change occurs so readily and rapidly that we must understand that our old conceptualizations about adolescence no longer fit the world in which teenagers live.

The Meaning of Success
Perhaps the essence of counseling teens is to assist them in developing their potential so that they can lead successful and fulfilled lives. But what is success? The lessons we learned in order to live effectively in *our* world may no longer be the lessons today's teens need.

A few years ago, the Stanford Research Institute studied three generations living in the middle-class range. The Institute wanted to learn the perceptions of each generation regarding symbols of success. Generally, the first generation would have been my parent's generation, people in their 60s and 70s. This generation lived through the Depression. They knew what it meant to have little. It appears their definition of success was largely determined by their experience of "going without." To them being successful meant that you did not have to go without *things.*

When asked what their symbols of success were, they listed things like a new car every year, a fancy house, a college degree, an executive position with a desk, a five-figure salary, and a three-week vacation every year. Their definition of success was in *having enough.*

The second generation studied by the Institute would closely parallel my own. I was a teenager in the 1950s. Most of my generation would be in their 40s. The symbols of success for this group did, in fact, include "things." You will notice from the list, however, that they would need more to be "successful" because their successful, Depression-era parents had already begun to accumulate things that were not available during the Depression. So this new generation already had things. What they needed in addition was *status.*

On their list of success symbols was an unlisted phone number, an office without a desk (a conference table instead), ownership of more than one home, a foreign car, a Swiss bank account, and frequent, unpredictable travel. This second generation defined success as *having the right stuff.*

The third generation, the generation that closely parallels teenagers in today's world, defined success to the Stanford researchers in a completely different way than did the preceeding groups. This generation defined success as people who are able to experience *free time* whenever they need it. To them, success integrates work and play. In my generation, you played only after the work was done. Teens have observed that, for my generation, the work is never done. They see successful people as playing-along-the-way. Furthermore, they defined success as more than monetary reward. A symbol of success for them is the person who is rewarded with honor and affection.

This generation further believes that a sign of success is to be able to express one's creativity. No wonder teens hate working at fast-food restaurants. My generation would say, "Hey, it's a job. And, you'll get $4.50 an hour." The teenager's internal, if not external response is, "Who cares?"

Additionally, this third group told the researchers that successful people are able to experience a full range of emotions and to have a wide range of interests and activities. Successful people, says this group, make major societal commitments in order to feel useful. Teenagers are moved by world hunger, peace, and the homeless.

Lastly, teens defined success as having good parenting skills, being philosophically independent, loving and being in touch with oneself, and having a strong spiritual connection.

In spite of the current reputation of teenagers as lazy, self-indulgent, and undisciplined, their list of success symbols is quite impressive. It makes my generation appear shallow, superficial, materialistic, and status-seeking. Essentially, teens have begun to define success as having more to do with *who you are* than what you do. They recognize that stuff and status don't guarantee fulfillment.

The point is that today's teens are being raised in a different world than their parents. Their motivations, values, and definition of success are qualitatively different. As adults who counsel kids, we need to recognize and respond to this fact.

A Different World
A couple of years ago, Jennifer James, an anthropologist, in a speech to the annual conference of the California Media and Library Edu-

cators Association, gave her listeners an interesting anthropological insight: We learn a unique set of survival skills by the age of ten.

What this means, of course, is that today's teenagers have learned a set of survival skills, based on what they need to know in order to survive the world in which they live. Those of us who attempt to counsel them need to understand clearly, therefore, the world that is uniquely theirs. Let's look at their world.

First, what we knew as the **traditional family** is an experience of a minority of today's teens. The traditional family had several key components: (1) the marriage of a husband and wife was the first and only marriage of either; (2) they were the biological parents of all the children residing in the home; (3) the husband worked outside the home; and (4) the wife worked in the home.

The large, **extended family** with parents, children, grandparents, aunts, uncles, and cousins has long been a thing of the past in our American culture. Today, however, even the **nuclear family** has been seriously challenged. In fact, only about thirty percent of today's teenagers live in a traditional, nuclear family setting.

Today's teenagers are more likely to live in families where a man and a woman marry, and each brings children from a previous marriage. Additionally, teens are likely to live in a two-career family, where both mother and father work outside the home. At the very least, many teens will live in a family setting in which at least one of the spouses has been married previously, maybe several times. Intact, traditional families are decreasing in numbers rapidly.

Today's teens, therefore, do not necessarily come from stable, secure, clearly defined families. They may be adjusting to the fact that they must build relationships with both of their biological parents, but this task must be done on an individual basis. Mom and Dad no longer come as a set. They may have several sets of grandparents. They may be much more self-sufficient due to the fact that both parents have jobs away from home. They may be surrounded by "family," but they are on their own for the most part.

The deterioration of the family unit is certainly a challenge for those adults working with youth. These teenagers do not always, if ever, have continuous guidance from parents who are asking other adults to assist them in the healthy development of their children. In many cases, youth leaders are providing parental functions to these young people: a supportive atmosphere, a caring heart, a compassionate ear, and a word of counsel.

There are, of course, teenagers who are fortunate enough to live in a strong, loving, secure, traditional family setting. But these young people come into contact with the thousands of other teens who don't. Even though these children experience a stable home, they must move in a world filled with children who know about separation, divorce, and **blended families.** Teens live in a world of confused, complex, ever-changing relationships. Significantly, a teenager's relationship with a youth leader may be the most dependable, reliable, trustworthy relationship he or she experiences.

Today's teens also live in a heterogenous society. Sociologists would call it a **pluralistic society.** In times past, the values of family, neighbors, school, and community were similar. If a teen were disciplined at school, he was likely to be disciplined at home as well. The teacher who disciplines a child at school in today's world is likely to hear from an irate parent, or at the very least, be questioned about the need for such behavior.

Pluralistic values and attitudes abound. The President of the United States supports an anti-drug campaign, and many teens' parents use drugs. We ask children to believe in the sanctity of life but stockpile enough nuclear armaments to destroy the world in minutes. Adults marry for life but divorce in a minute. No wonder it is the norm for teens to take longer to sort life out.

Youth leaders used to play a supportive role to parents as they taught spiritual and cultural values to adolescents. Now these same leaders plead for the support of parents as they attempt to lead children to higher values. In all of this confusion, it is the aim of the counselor to help bring clarity, order, and congruence to the lives of teenagers! It is a tremendous challenge, but the rewards are tremendous.

Another fact of today's world is that teenagers aren't needed as they were in the past. Previous generations of teenagers worked on family farms or in small family businesses. Teens were viewed as being important because they were important! They did chores, they did real work, they helped the family make money. My wife, for example, worked in her family's candy store on the main street of the small Colorado town where they lived. Her job was significant. She waited on the customers who came in to buy the family's product.

Can you imagine the sense of self-esteem she must have felt as her parents gave her such responsibility? She received a constant message from her family that she was important and of value to them. She knew, without a doubt, that her family needed her.

In contrast, I was talking to a teenager who was looking for a job. I asked him how his search was going. "Terrible," he said. "Either they want to pay you minimum wage for a meaningless job, or you aren't qualified to do anything." Today's teenagers struggle to feel significant and useful.

As a counselor, you can help teenagers become aware of their unique contribution to you and to other teens. Perhaps you have a teenager in your group who simply makes meetings better because of her enthusiasm, or her maturity, or the fact that she just brings out the best in those around her. Tell her. Say something like, "Maria, thanks for coming tonight. Our group really benefits from your energy. It's not the same when you're not around."

Maria, no doubt, will hear what you are really saying: "I need you." She can then experience herself as an asset, making a significant contribution to your life and others.

In today's world, teenagers are faced with thousands of choices that were unheard of a generation ago. Sifting and sorting through these possibilities can take a lot of time and can be overwhelming to the decision-maker. Late adolescent women of a generation ago had a fairly clear view of their career potential. They could be teachers, nurses, secretaries, or housewives. Today's career directions are unlimited for these women, and it isn't any easier for men.

Most adults have experienced the difficulty of moving in a direction when overwhelmed by too many choices. For me, a bookstore enables me to know what it must be like for teenagers in today's world of unlimited possibilities. I visit bookstores often, and frequently leave without a book. Not because I'm disinterested; I just don't have time to narrow down my choices in the short time I have.

For teenagers, however, it's even worse than my bookstore experiences. I don't *have* to buy a book, and few people care if I do. For teens, everyone asks them constantly about their plans. "Are you going to college after high school graduation?" "What will your major be?" "What do you think you want to do?" "Do you have a career picked out?" And these are just the questions that relate to careers!

Most teenagers will eventually make their way through this maze. It's interesting, however, that a few don't. Occasionally, when they reach young adulthood, they are so confused that they suffer from what mental health professionals diagnose as an identity disorder. It is believed that a significant contributor to this disorder is the fact that so many choices must be made in order for a person to evolve a clear self-identity.

The development of identity is still composed of three major facets: personal, social, and career. One's personal identity centers on the question, "Who am I?" The teen's strengths, weaknesses, values, priorities, and faith help determine the answer to this question. The second facet, social identity, focuses on the question, "How do I relate to others, and how do others relate to me?" The kind of people teenagers like, how they resolve conflict with peers and adults, and their behavior with the opposite sex all contribute to answering this second question. The third facet, career identity, centers on the question, "What am I going to do with the rest of my life?"

The process of answering these questions is unique to today's adolescents because of the complexity of the world in which they live. The consequences of such a complicated world are poor focus, lack of direction, procrastination, and protracted decision-making. In this myriad of details the counselor tries to help the teenager clear a path toward an appropriate goal.

The counselor who can see the potential of a young man or woman can assist in sorting through all the possible choices and directions. The teen will eventually make the choices, but the youth leader who serves as counselor can assist in the process of arriving at these important and significant decisions.

Trends of the Future

As counselors who have grown up in a different world than today's teenagers, what are the trends that we need to know in order to enter their world? Jennifer James, in her presentation to her audience of library educators, identified several significant trends that counselors must know to enter the world of today's teens:

1. There is less desire for quantity of things and more demand for quality of life.
2. There is less appreciation for the person who is tough, self-sufficient, and in control, and more appreciation for the sensitive, empathetic, connected person.
3. There is a decrease in the use of control as a method of managing others and an increase in a management style that involves everyone in the decision-making process.
4. There is less importance being placed on "doing" and more importance being placed on "being."
5. There is less enjoyment being derived from observing others (sporting events) and more enjoyment being derived from participating personally (jogging, aerobics).
6. There is less emphasis on sex as a fulfilling activity in and of itself and more emphasis on how sex relates to closeness and intimacy in relationships.
7. There is less emphasis being placed on work and more emphasis being placed on play.
8. There are fewer instances in which only a few choices are available and more instances in which multiple options are available.
9. There are fewer people espousing atheism and greater interest in spiritual things (not necessarily Christian).
10. There is less interest and need for status but much emphasis on equality and community.

The task of helping teenagers in today's world is greater than it has ever been. But the rewards too, are greater! When you offer to come alongside a teen, you never have to question whether your time was spent meaningfully. Think of it. You are helping teenagers become the very people God created them to be!

Five

GROWTH GOALS
OF TEENAGERS

Adults who find today's teenagers disconcerting often view the goal
of adolescence as being little more than *surviving* the period, as
though reaching the age of twenty has significance in and of itself.

This perspective of adolescence sees the teen years as a period to
be tolerated, as though the victor is one who overcomes several
years of misfortune. It's the misguided idea that leaving the teen
years automatically brings resolution and peace to the problems and
conflicts of the preceding years. There are even those—some in the
Christian community—who object to and refuse to use the term
"adolescence" when describing youngsters in this age-span. They
prefer to use the term "teenager" exclusively, which is a chronologi-
cal indicator but does not carry with it the significance of what is
occurring during these years.

Interestingly, the term "teenager" is somewhat inaccurate if we
are talking about these young people in a developmental sense. The
significant growth and development of this period sometimes begins

before age thirteen and often continues into the middle twenties.

David Elkind discusses the early development of children in his book, *The Hurried Child.* Elkind says, "Today's pressures on middle-class children to grow up fast begins in early childhood." He further says, "When children are expected to dress, act, and think as adults, they are really being asked to playact, because all the trappings of adulthood do not in any way make them adults. . . . "

On the other hand, Susan Littwin, in her book *The Postponed Generation,* discusses the fact that adulthood is being postponed or delayed so that adolescent issues are often not fully resolved until the young person is in his mid-twenties.

Recently I had lunch with a national leader of Young Life, an organization that ministers to teenagers. We were talking about the fact that the mission of Young Life originally focused on the high school student. During the past few years, in response to the fact that teens begin the process of growing up much earlier, Young Life has begun to minister to the early adolescent in junior high school.

As we talked, however, we realized that young people who had graduated from high school aren't necessarily beyond the need for an organization that continues to work with them until they have reached maturity. Finally, this committed youth leader conceptualized the problem we now face when trying to pinpoint our target population. "Never have kids experienced adult issues so early and yet taken so long to integrate them." He was saying that kids begin to grow up during childhood but can't get it all together until their mid-twenties.

A period that begins so early and lasts so long surely has significance beyond the mere counting of years. The successful maneuvering through this period certainly is evaluated by more than the attainment of age twenty. The truth of the matter is that this age-span (twelve to twenty) serves as a dynamic, significant, sometimes tumultuous passage from childhood to adulthood.

Our word adolescence comes from the Latin word *adolescens* which means "growing up." Although this is the "work" of young people in their teen years, it isn't particularly easy. Guy LeFrancois said it well in his book, *Of Children.* "Because Western culture does not tell its children when they have become men and women, they must discover it for themselves. And the discovery is made particularly difficult by the fact that the culture training them is continuous—that is, there is no clear demarcation of passage from one state to another."

The counselor of teens who recognizes and appreciates that adolescence serves a unique developmental function, the making of mature adults from what once were children, will be in a position to effectively help today's young people to traverse this significant passage.

Part of the essence of maturity is being a "whole" person. Various elements of our physical selves and personalities are integrated in such a way that we become unique persons. We can use our "whole selves" to love, to be productive, to reach goals. It is during adolescence that the integration process takes place.

Physical Development

Developmental psychologists use two terms to indicate the beginning of adolescence. The first is **pubescence,** which refers to all of the changes that occur in late childhood and early adolescence. Most of us are well aware of the physical and sexual changes which occur because we experienced these changes. For girls, there is the appearance of pubic hair, the enlargement of breasts, a rapid growth spurt, sweat gland development, the first menstrual period (referred to as menarche), and the appearance of underarm hair.

For boys, there is the appearance of pubic hair, the enlargement of the testes, a rapid growth spurt, sweat gland development, the lowering of the voice, the appearance of a beard, underarm hair, and, less frequently, chest hair. They also develop the ability to ejaculate semen.

The second term used to indicate the start of adolescence is **puberty.** Most frequently, in fact, adolescence is defined as the period between puberty and adulthood. Whereas pubescence refers to the changes leading to sexual maturity, puberty indicates sexual maturity. For example, the occurrence of a girl's first menstrual period at pubescence does not indicate fertility. In spite of menarche, girls typically do not become fertile for another year. At puberty, however, fertility has been achieved.

Teenagers, therefore, become physically and sexually mature before they become mature in other areas. In a way, they are initially children trying to catch up to their adult bodies. Teenagers do not "decide" to grow up. They are thrust into the growing up process due to hormonal changes that lead to physical and sexual maturity.

Naturally, this whole process, although common to all, is unique in terms of timetable. All teens experience all of the aforementioned changes to one degree or another, but one early adolescent may mature sexually in junior high school, while another teen may not mature until high school. Typically, girls mature sooner, but boys (to their relief) catch up.

If youth workers are familiar with these changes, why is it so important to focus on them in order to increase one's effectiveness as a counselor? There are several reasons.

• *First, as a counselor, it is always important to know where a teenager is developmentally.* Where they are determines their issues, their concerns, their fears, their challenges. Prior to these dynamic physical and sexual changes, youngsters are children dealing with childhood issues. But, when puberty begins, the task of the counselor is to assist teenagers in understanding and adjusting to these changes, all of which impact their sense of self, their relational patterns, and all other areas of their development.

The onset of puberty, therefore, sets the counselor's agenda when working with teens. Issues such as identity, the importance of peers, separation from parents, and career choices are just around the corner. Prior to puberty, these issues are premature areas of concern for the counselor.

• *Second, teenagers are generally uncertain about all of these changes.* Kids in elementary school are "put together" fairly well. They are generally coordinated and accepting of their physical presence. Their growth has been relatively slow, uniform, and steady. Suddenly and unexpectedly, these youngsters experience a rapid growth spurt, and this growth may not be uniform at all. Paul Mussen, in the book *Psychological Development: A Life-Span Approach,* says, "The average adolescent is unusually sensitive to and often critical of his or her changing physical self." He continues, "If adolescents are asked what they like or dislike about themselves, physical characteristics are typically mentioned more often than either social or intellectual ones."

Robert Coles and Geoffrey Stokes in their book *Sex and the American Teenager,* quote a teenage girl. "When will it end — so we can just have a body that looks the same, from one week to another?" Teenagers worry greatly about these changes, and if they are too different from their peers, these changes can be a source of poor self-esteem.

• *Third, teenagers who develop early or late are particularly self-conscious.* Teens who are changing along with everyone else at least have the consolation that it is happening to everyone else. That makes it easier. For those at the extremes of the timetable, however, it can be particularly painful. The early-developing girl wants to hide her breasts while taking a shower in her physical education class, while the late-developing girl is afraid she will never develop breasts. It is just as painful for boys. The early- and late-developing boys are teased unmercifully by other guys. Once again, those of us who have the opportunity to counsel with teens can play a tremendously reassuring role by reminding teens that, in the end, we all complete satisfactorily the development process.

Mental Development

The ability to think abstractly is a developed mental process. Small children are not able to conceptualize complicated thoughts or ideas. That's why we use Santa Claus to explain the concept of generosity. We are not trying to be deceitful; we simply know that children can better relate to a kindly, warm-hearted old man who likes to give gifts.

While older children have the ability to think logically, their thinking patterns are centered on concrete facts and observations. For this reason, Jean Piaget, one of history's foremost authorities on the development of the intellect, labeled the thinking of children between the ages of seven and eleven as **concrete operations.** These children can organize facts, understand classification systems, and do arithmetic problems.

It isn't until adolescence, somewhere between the ages of eleven and fifteen, that young people begin to develop the ability to think about abstract ideas. Such thinking enables them to compare and contrast the "ideal" with the "real," to develop and test hypotheses, to think about the future, to understand complex concepts and contrary-to-fact propositions. Piaget called this stage of intellectual development **formal operations.** This means that teenagers think like adults. It is true that they may not arrive at the same conclusions as adults, but this is usually due to different perceptions, different priorities, or a lack of experience. Their process of thinking, however, is the same as mature adults.

Teenagers can plan, analyze, evaluate, and hypothesize. They can play "What if . . . ?" The fact that they can reason means they no longer desire to follow directions submissively (if they ever did)! They have ideas of their own on matters of interest to them. They may consider the views of their parents and other adults, but they do not necessarily want our answers. They often take the opposite side of an argument, just to find out what it feels like.

Obviously, these new thinking skills require that adults significantly change the manner in which they relate to these young people. Parents, having chosen what was best for their children for years, may have a difficult time making this adjustment. It is much easier for a counselor to relate to teenagers who think like adults. Counselors don't tell kids what to do. They assist teenagers in using these new intellectual skills to consider, explore, and understand the complex issues of life as they develop their own perception of themselves as adults and embrace a lifestyle that is worthy of commitment.

Emotional Development
Anyone who works with teens recognizes their tendency to experience mood swings. They can be elated, depressed, hopeful, angry, restful, restless — all within a few hours! If this were the case with an adult, a mental health professional would describe the person's emotionality as **labile.** This could very likely be a sign of psychopathology, where the adult's emotional responses are unstable and inappropriate to the actual, external circumstances.

With adolescents, however, we do not describe mood swings as an emotional lability. We describe them as age-appropriate, normal, typical, expected behavior of individuals in this age-span. Although mood swings of adolescents when accompanied by certain other symptoms (personality change, drastic change of behavior, dilation of pupils, disinterest in school, among others) may indicate drug use, mood swings alone are expected among teenagers.

A few years ago, I learned of a late adolescent who had recently graduated from high school. On the day he was to move off to college, his dad found him in his room, halfheartedly packing his clothes and belongings. He seemed discouraged and irritable. His dad remarked, "Son, what's the matter? I thought this would have been the happiest day of your life."

This adolescent told how it was quite clearly. "I kind of liked my life. I knew everybody. I'm comfortable with where I live. I know what I'm doing. But they're making me change my whole life." And then with a sense of resignation he said, "As far as I'm concerned, my life is over!"

His father inwardly chuckled. Here was a young man with all of life ahead of him. He was about to attend a small, caring, Christian college in one of the most attractive locations of any college in America. His dorm was a few hundred yards from the edge of the Pacific Ocean. His family was paying for his room, board, and tuition. For this inexperienced adolescent, however, it was all unknown territory. Therefore, life was over for him.

In a matter of a few hours, the family drove to his dorm. As this new college freshman climbed reluctantly out of the car, a smiling, excited, energetic co-ed yelled, "Danny! You're going here? I didn't know that. Wow!" It was a girl from his high school.

The two of them were off in a flash, leaving his mom and dad to carry the luggage into the dorm. Loaded down with all their son's stuff, they found him in the dorm lounge, looking at a vending machine. He put in his money and took out a soft drink. He took a big swallow and said, "Ah, Dr. Pepper. Life is good!"

From "Life is over" to "Life is good," all in a matter of hours. Crazy? For adults, yes. For teenagers, it's normal. So, why the mood swings? For the most part, adolescents lack experience. When things are down, when their decisions go awry, when circumstances aren't what they expected, they lack the experience to know that their situation is temporary. When they break up with a romantic interest, for example, they aren't at all sure that there will ever be another. They have too little experience, so they have nothing to moderate their emotional responses.

Mood swings, however, are not the key to understanding the emotional development of teenagers. Emotionally mature adults have a sense of who they are. They are aware of their strengths and limitations, and they are comfortable with each. They are familiar with their own internal resources; they are resilient in the face of obstacles or tragedy; and they have a sense that, as much as is possible, they control their own destiny.

The emotional developmental task for teenagers is to learn who they are apart from their parents. They begin this process of wanting to make their own decisions, to "get in touch" with their feelings, to choose their own friends, to play various roles to see how they feel, to take the opposite side of an argument with their parents, to spend time alone. All these experiences are for the purpose of developing a sense of self.

Unfortunately, many adults want to know "What happened to Johnny? He used to be such a nice boy." Well, nothing has happened to Johnny, if we understand the work he is doing: becoming an emotionally mature adult, responsible for himself and committed to significant others he cares about. On the other hand, everything is happening to Johnny. *He is growing up!*

The counselor of teenagers is in a challenging position to help them explore who they are apart from their parents in an environment that is relatively safe and secure. It is a substantive and fulfilling task to help them take more and more responsibility for themselves, to help them pick up the pieces after poor decisions have been made, to help them discern their uniqueness and value, and to help them figure out constructive and positive patterns of relating to their friends.

Social Development

Adolescence is the time when adult social skills are learned. This process of socialization enlightens us as to the reason peer relationships are so important to teenagers. Knowing how to make others comfortable, to "small talk," to respond to a compliment, to cooperatively plan an event, to relate to someone different, to assert an opinion, to initiate a relationship, to express a feeling—all these are social skills which must be learned. And the peer group is the context in which these skills are learned.

Parents, of course, spend hours trying to teach their children how to act in social situations. We teach our kids table manners, how to say thank you, how to speak respectfully to adults. These are skills that need to be taught. But being a child responding to adults in somewhat ritualized situations is not the same as being with others your own age, in which the dynamics of what is going on are ever changing before your very eyes!

Several years ago, in a moment of vulnerability, an adult friend of mine told me, "You know, I have often been at a loss as to how I should act in social situations. For years, I thought I was just different, or, that something was wrong with me. It seemed like everybody else knew what was going on or what to do. Recently, however, I have come to realize that I never had the opportunity to learn social skills when I was growing up."

Fortunately for this man, he is making up for lost time. His plight, however, need not happen to the teenagers we counsel. Socialization is a large part of what adolescence is all about. It is a transition period in which teenagers learn how to behave and respond to others with adult maturity.

The heart of counseling is a relationship. As we work with teens who struggle with the complex social skills required for our society, we are modeling in our relationship with them the very skills they need. What they learn in their relationship with us can be used as they relate to other significant adults and peers in their lives.

Moral Development

A sense of morality, like every other area of development, seems to occur in stages. Lawrence Kohlberg, building on the original work of Jean Piaget, developed a three-level, six-stage theory of moral development. Generally, the lowest level relates to children, who are interested in their own needs and the consequences of their behavior. Kohlberg's second level, the **conventional level,** is the level at which most early adolescents have developed a sense of morality.

Within the conventional level, which has two stages, young adolescents are interested in how they should behave. The first stage is known as the *good boy, good girl orientation.* As we work with early adolescents, it is easy to see that these young people are always concerned with winning the approval of their peers and certain significant adults. Doing what pleases others is at the core of their moral reasoning. Their behavior is "conventional" in that it is behavior that most people support.

As teenagers become middle- and late-adolescents, they are generally found at the second stage of the conventional level. Kohlberg identified this stage as a *law and order orientation.* Teenagers in this stage recognize the need for social order, and they accept some responsibility for doing their part in keeping such order. They recognize that all rules have limitations, but that having no rules leads to chaos. They may even try to change what they believe to be unjust rules.

The most highly developed teenagers in late adolescence reach the first stage of the third level, the **principled level,** of moral reasoning. This first stage, called the *social contract orientation,* defines morality as respect for the rights of others and the honoring of agreements and contracts between people. Behavior is not simply motivated because everyone feels good as a result, but behavior is centered on a principle, whether or not one receives personal gain.

For example, a teenager takes a test during first period at school. She is asked for the test questions by someone who will take the same exam during third period. The person asking for the questions is someone the girl really wants as a friend. She is tempted to help this girl because she thinks it will help win this girl's favor. In the end, despite the fact that she may jeopardize her relationship with this other girl, she refuses to give out the test questions because it wouldn't be fair to others. Respecting the right of all students to have an equal chance of doing well on the test has become her guide in making her decision.

Few older adolescents (and adults) go beyond this social contract orientation, according to Kohlberg. Anyone doing so would reach what has been called the *universal ethical principle orientation.* This orientation is probably the goal of most Christians. At its essence, this stage defines morality on the basis of behavior that is centered on an abstract principle such as the Golden Rule, "Do unto others what you would have them do unto you."

Teenagers often seek a counselor when faced with a moral dilemma. And teenagers face many moral decisions. "Do I report a friend who is selling drugs?" "Do I tell a friend's parents that their daughter is talking about getting an abortion?" "Do I look at test questions that are being circulated?" "Do I write a paper for a friend who is failing a class?" "Do I change the grades on my report card because I will lose the use of my car if I don't?" "Do I snub a friend in front of the in-crowd when members of the clique don't accept him?" The counselor can assist teenagers significantly by helping them clarify their values, set priorities, and make decisions of integrity. This process is particularly difficult for adolescents due to their need to conform in order to assure approval from their peers. Support and affirmation from a counselor can help teens make these difficult decisions.

Faith Development

James Fowler, in his book *Stages of Faith,* suggests that faith is developed through a series of identifiable stages. He outlines one pre-stage and six stages, covering the entire age-span of development. It is in the third stage, called **synthetic-conventional faith,** that most teenagers reside.

The faith level of most teens is defined in terms of interpersonal relationships with others. That's why it is called "conventional" faith. The faith of adolescents, for example, is not so much a personal faith as it is a "group" faith. Rather than what *I* believe, it is what *we* believe.

53

Fowler says that one's faith arises out of one's sense of identity. Teenagers, as we have noted, are still working on a sense of self. Their development is not clear or strong enough yet to support a personal faith that is based on an independent perspective. An adolescent's faith is typically a "conformist" perspective, based on the beliefs and expectations of significant adults and peers.

The stage of faith that follows the synthetic-conventional stage is called **individuative-reflective faith.** This level of faith development defines faith in more personal terms. This is made possible by the development of a strong self-identity, which supports a more independent perspective. Interestingly, Fowler suggests that few adults develop beyond the stage in which most teenagers are found.

Helping teenagers begin to develop a more personal faith may be a high priority for the counselor working with an early adolescent who shows particular maturity in things of a spiritual nature. Typically, however, it will likely be the late adolescent who wants to explore elements of a personal faith with the counselor.

The Unity of Development
There is a wonderful, synergistic nature to development. In other words, each element of development has a wholeness in itself, and yet each element is a meaningful part of the whole. For example, physical and sexual maturity, complete in themselves, are also important components to the founding of the teen's identity. Identity directly affects the possibility of developing faith at the individuative-reflective level. A personal faith and a sense of morality are based on abstract ideas which are understood because of the teen's ability to think abstractly, a stage of mental development. The need to conform, a part of a teen's level of socialization, impacts faith development.

Each element of development influences and is influenced by every other area of growth. We can only stand in awe as we watch a child become a mature adult! God created us with the capacity to grow, and nowhere is growth more evident than during adolescence. It is in this dynamic, life-changing passage toward maturity that the counselor enters the lives of teenagers.

Six

GETTING TEENAGERS TO TALK

Speaking to a group of parents one day, I remarked that I suspected that the lower jaws of teenagers don't work. Suddenly, the entire audience broke out in laughter. That's because every parent has experienced what it is like when teenagers really don't want to talk. Their answers are barely audible and almost unintelligible. Many parents are long-suffering, however, so they repeat their questions, thinking their hearing is deteriorating. Once again, the responses they hear may be jumbled murmurs or grunts!

At other times, it appears as though teens have an aversion to using complete sentences. Instead, they can only answer in one-word statements. A parent might ask, "How was school today?"

The adolescent answers, "Fine."

"Oh," says the parent. "What happened?"

The teenager answers, "Nothing."

With some irritation creeping into his tone, the parent persists. "Well, did you learn anything new today?"

"No," says the teen.

"Well, you must have some homework," suggests the parent.

"Nope," answers the teen. With a great sense of elaboration, he continues, "I did it all at school."

Getting a teenager to talk can be a challenge, not just for parents, but counselors as well. In order to be an effective counselor, those who work with young people must find ways to facilitate open communication between themselves and teenagers. There is nothing quite so uncomfortable to most adults as trying to get kids to open up when they refuse to do so. Awkward silences, one-word sentences, or shrugs of the shoulders can be frustrating, if not irritating to the counselor.

When my son was 16 or 17 years old, my family was on an outing with another family. We were traveling in their station wagon. My wife, the wife of the other couple, and I were seated on the middle seat of the car. In the back seat were the other couple's children. My son was sitting in the front seat with the husband of the other couple.

As we drove, I was listening to the two women beside me, occasionally responding to their conversation. In the midst of their conversation, I overheard my friend in the front seat ask my son a question. "So, Dan, do you have a special girl?"

It was such a direct question that I inwardly laughed and thought, *Dan will never answer that question!*

To my surprise, I heard my son answer, "Well, as a matter of fact, I do."

Then my friend asked, "Did you just meet her, or have you had your eye on her for quite a while?"

By this time, I was figuratively on the edge of my seat to hear what was going to happen next.

"I've had my eye on her for quite awhile," answered my son.

Then my friend responded, "That's great, Dan! She must be really something."

Finally, my son reverted to a one-word answer, "Yeah!"

What was this adult's secret? Are there identifiable differences between people who can get teens to talk and those who can't? Are there approaches that encourage and facilitate open communication between adults and teenagers? Yes. Anyone who wants to counsel teenagers will want to be familiar with those attitudes and communication patterns that make it easy for teenagers to open up.

What Gets in the Way?

Before we examine approaches that facilitate openness among teens, it may be helpful to identify those communciation patterns that *hinder* the process of talking to teenagers. Thomas Gordon, in his book *Parent Effectiveness Training*, was one of the first professional therapists to address this problem. Essentially, he made a distinction between what he calls *language of acceptance* and *language of unacceptance.* Says Gordon, "Most parents rely heavily on the language of unacceptance in rearing children, believing this is the best way to help them. The soil that most parents provide for their children's growth is heavy with evaluation, judgment, criticism, preaching, moralizing, admonishing, and commanding—messages that convey unacceptance of the child as he is."

Obviously, there are times when parents must evaluate, admonish, and command. These functions, however, are not for the purpose of getting children or teenagers to talk. As Gordon says, "The language of unacceptance turns kids off. They stop talking to their parents. They learn that it is far more comfortable to keep their feelings and problems to themselves."

Although Gordon was speaking to parents, his message to them came out of the experience of professional counselors. Anything that smacks of disapproval, judgment, criticism, or ridicule hinders teenagers from communicating to adults freely.

Facilitating Talk through Acceptance

Although we have spoken previously about the need for a counselor to have unconditional positive regard for counselees, this characteristic must be communicated and demonstrated before a teenager will talk.

Generally, a counselor's acceptance of a teenager is communicated in tone and content. It can be demonstrated verbally or nonverbally. In the example of my son talking about his girlfriend, my friend did not preface his opening question by telling my son that he was accepted for who he was. His tone was matter-of-fact when he asked whether a special girl was in the picture. The message was between the lines. He was saying, "The idea that you would have a girlfriend is perfectly plausible to me. I would expect you to be attractive to girls. On the other hand, if you don't, that doesn't change the fact."

This adult friend also communicated a *genuine* interest as he asked his questions. He sounded and appeared as though he really wanted to know how Dan was doing in the "girl department." Teens detest being patronized. They are not interested in becoming vulnerable if adults seem not to care. Sincerity makes a tremendous impact on teenagers because they somewhat expect parents and other adults not to take them seriously.

Adults who communicate a more positive message have half the battle won. Suddenly, teens move their jaws, speak in full sentences, volunteer information, and speak so they can be heard. When adolescents feel valued and respected, they communicate freely, naturally, and willingly.

Verbal Communication of Acceptance

One of the most obvious ways to communicate acceptance is to speak in language that is free of your own agendas, thoughts, feelings, and judgments. The words you use do make a difference in the clear communication of acceptance. Here are some phrases that communicate acceptance and encourage a teenager to talk:

"I'd like to hear what you think about that."

"Tell me more."

"Yes, go on."

"It sounds like you feel strongly about this."

"How do you feel?"

"Would you like to talk about it?"

"Start from the beginning."

These phrases are often called **door openers.** They serve to get a teenager started. They communicate the fact that the counselor is ready to listen with a completely objective and open stance. They communicate respect and appreciation for the adolescent's point of view. They don't just open the door to conversation, however, they also encourage a teenager to continue. By using such phrases, the counselor is saying, "I have time. This is important because what you are saying is important to *you.*"

Nonverbal Communication of Acceptance

There are times when one's behavior is a more powerful expression of acceptance than words. For example, I often suggest that a teenager sit in my chair in my counseling office. I then sit on the sofa. I am trying to communicate the idea that I am not superior, nor do I need to control the situation. Hopefully, teenagers in my office recognize that it is not my purpose to make them do something they don't want to do. I am saying, "I'm here for you if I can be of some help."

Remember that my son sat in the front seat of my friend's car. In family outings, particularly when a station wagon is the mode of transportation, the children usually sit in the backseat. My friend, however, invited Dan to sit up front with him. The front seat is usually reserved for adults. The opportunity to sit in the front seat communicated a powerful message to this young, emerging adult: "I'm special to this adult." It was therefore easier for him to communicate freely, without fear of rejection, criticism, or judgment.

There are many ways a youth worker who counsels teens can communicate acceptance in a nonverbal way. Some examples are as follows:

- Look a teenager in the eye when he is talking to you.
- Give a teenager your full attention when in conversation.
- Refrain from looking at your watch every few minutes, as

though something else is more important.

- Refrain from talking to a teenager with your desk between the two of you. Such an arrangement puts you in an "authority" position.
- Use facial expressions and gestures that communicate openness and invite a teenager to "come closer."
- Allow a teenager to solve his or her problem. This communicates the message, "I believe in you."
- Be quiet, say nothing, just listen.
- Resist the tendency to tell a teen's parents the content of your conversation unless the adolescent's welfare is in jeopardy.

Let's look at two examples of a counselor talking to a teenager. The first scenario is one in which the language of unacceptance is present.

Counselor: "So, do you have a special girl?"

Teenager: "Well, as a matter of fact I do."

Counselor: "I'm sure she is a Christian. Where does she go to church?"

Teenager: "I don't know."

Counselor: "Haven't you asked her? You sure wouldn't want to go with a girl that isn't a Christian, would you?"

Teenager: "I guess not. I'm hungry. When are we going to eat?"

Naturally, it is desirable for a young teen to have a girlfriend who shares his same faith and values. The counselor's purpose at the moment, however, is to get this young man to talk. The conversation begins well enough, but almost immediately the counselor inserts an agenda that changes the nature of the moment. The teenager quickly closes down and changes the subject.

Let's look at a second scenario in which the counselor facilitates communication and still is concerned about the young man's choices.

Counselor: "So, do you have a special girl?"

Teenager: "Well, as a matter of fact I do."

Counselor: "That's great! Tell me how you met her."

Teenager: "At school. We have several classes together."

Counselor: "Man, I'd love to meet her. Can you bring her to our youth group?"

Teenager: "I don't know. I don't think she goes to church."

Counselor: "Maybe she'd come on our ski trip."

Teenager: "Really? That'd be great. I really like her. My parents won't approve of her if they find out she doesn't go to church. I didn't know what to do."

Counselor: "Sure. Why don't you invite her."

Notice that the counselor in this scenario respects this teenager's right to choose his girlfriend and is sensitive to his feelings about her. There is no disapproval in his tone or the content of his responses. As a consequence, the counselor begins to know the importance this young man places on his new relationship and becomes aware of this teen's potential conflict with his parents. At the same time that this counselor gives gentle support, a suggestion is given that might provide this young man with a way to invite his girlfriend to church. Finally, this teenager is made aware that his non-Christian girlfriend is welcome in the youth group.

Perhaps what is most important about the second dialogue, however, is the fact that the counselor paved the way for future talks with this young man. This teen realizes that he can share what he thinks and feels without fear of rejection. It wouldn't be surprising at all for this teen to *initiate* future discussion with the counselor as his relationship grows with his girlfriend, and as he attempts to deal with the fact that she is from an unchurched home. The dialogue remains open.

The Teen's Timing

It is typical for adults to determine the schedule of children. And, when children become teenagers, adults tend to continue the process of choosing when they are to talk. The problem, however, is that none of us, teens or adults alike, can always be ready or willing to talk on cue. Sometimes we don't have time to adequately talk about something that is important. Or, we are not sure yet just what we think or feel about a matter. So discussion is premature. There are times when we are too tired to talk and other times when we choose not to make public a thought or feeling that we hold as private. As adults, we have the right to determine, at least to some degree, when is the best time to talk. And, when we are ready, we have no problem in talking.

The same can be said for teens. Frankly, although verbal and non-verbal language can facilitate discussion, there will be times when teens do not want to talk. Effective counselors allow teens to be an important factor in determining when they want to share. They have learned that when a teenager *wants* to talk, it is difficult to get them to stop! In times like these talking to teens is effortless.

It would be rare for the teenager to stop and say, "Hey, I'm ready to talk now." Usually, they begin talking easily within the context of what is going on around them. A few years ago, for example, my wife and I were relaxing in our spa with our son. After a while, my wife went into the house. My son and I were left in the spa. He began to talk . . . and talk . . . and talk. Evidently I was so relaxed that I didn't say much of anything. I just listened.

Suddenly I thought, "This is incredible. He is telling me everything that is currently important to him. If I just keep my mouth shut, I'll really know what's going on in his life." At the time, of course, I was not functioning as a counselor. I was a father listening to my son. The point, however, is that teens often initiate talking when the setting and environment seem right to them. Often we miss a chance because we are so busy determining when *we* want them to talk or deciding when *we* want to listen. When the counselor is attentive to those moments when the teen chooses to talk, the counseling process becomes much easier. It isn't always possible to set aside previous priorities, but when we can, the results can be very productive.

Effective counselors not only are attentive to the moment when a teen chooses to talk, but he or she also makes note of the setting, time, and circumstances that were a part of a facilitative environment. For example, some teens might only open up when they are in a one-on-one relationship with the counselor. Others might need the support of a peer. A few might open up when involved in a project, while others might need particular encouragement to talk. Reproducing circumstances that help a particular teen talk is within the counselor's ability. It is impossible to "make" a teenager talk, but a good counselor recognizes that it is a part of the counseling process to create an environment that makes talking easier for teenagers.

A Zest for Life

Recently a national youth organization completed an informal survey regarding the primary characteristic teens want in a youth leader. What would you think that one characteristic would be? Wisdom, leadership, spiritual maturity? It was none of these. Teenagers want their youth worker to be "someone who is fun to be with."

This really isn't too surprising. Most of us want to be around enjoyable people. Our schedules are busy, there are enough toxic people in our lives, and our energy levels are limited. Therefore we are more likely to want to spend our time with people who add joy to our lives.

Naturally, it is easier to talk when the environment we're in is warm, relaxed, playful. Our defenses go down, our barriers are removed, our talk grows more spontaneous. For teenagers, self-disclosure is less threatening in such an environment. Counseling, of course, can and should be about significant issues. But it is easier to cry after we have laughed.

Helpful counselors realize that much of life for teenagers is serious business to them. So their defenses are up. They hide their vulnerabilities, ignorance, fears, and conflicts. It is laughter, however, that enables them to feel safe — and to become vulnerable. In the seriousness of counseling, teenagers still want to be with someone who is "fun." The consequence is that talk is more spontaneous and free. Take teenagers seriously, but don't take life too seriously. Teenagers are then apt to gravitate toward you. They will also be more likely to talk to you!

The Key Factor

The most important factor that encourages a teenager to talk is being a good listener. *People talk to those who will listen.* That's why it is so essential for the counselor to realize what makes counseling a unique process. If we want to talk, then we rap, advise, teach, or preach. It isn't that we don't talk in counseling, but *we listen first, and talk second.* In the other roles, we generally talk first, and listen in order that we might respond to questions.

Some people mistakenly believe that listening is always a passive activity. It can be, but **passive listening** is characterized by silence. **Active listening,** on the other hand, is a process of being fully involved in what a speaker is saying. It requires that the listener *decode* what is being said as accurately as possible. This may require intense focus, rewording, clarification, feedback, and correction.

Thomas Gordon, in his book *Parent Effectiveness Training,* defines active listening in the following manner:

> In active listening, then, the receiver tries to understand what it is the sender is feeling or what his message means. Then he puts his understanding into his own words (code) and feeds it back for the sender's verification. The receiver does not send a message of his own—such as an evaluation, opinion, advice, logic, analysis, or question. He feeds back only what he feels the sender's message meant—nothing more, nothing less.

The exhaustion and burnout that professional counselors experience is related partially to this process of listening. It takes energy to focus intently on a sender's message and understand its meaning accurately. The lay counselor will probably not have to listen as many hours as the professional counselor does, but the ingredients of the active listening process are the same.

Let's look at an example of active listening:

Counselor: "How's it going?"

Teenager: "Oh, OK, I guess." (Tone sounds discouraged.)

Counselor: "You sound a bit down."

Teenager: "I guess I am."

Counselor: "Do you want to talk about it?"

Teenager: "It's my parents. They just don't understand me."

Counselor: "You're discouraged about your relationship with them."

Teenager: "Yeah. We just don't get along."

Counselor: "Mm-hmmm."

Teenager: "It seems like I can never please them. Nobody could."

Counselor: "Pleasing them is important to you."

Teenager: "Well, sure. Wouldn't you want to please your parents at least once in a while? They're the most critical parents I know."

Counselor: "It really hurts when they criticize you."

Teenager: "I feel . . . I feel . . . "

Counselor: "You feel . . . "

Teenager: "Like they don't care about me. Sometimes I hate them."

Counselor: "Their lack of positive response has made you so mad that you hate them."

Teenager: "I don't really hate them . . . but I get so discouraged. Why should I even try?"

Counselor: "You feel like giving up."

Teenager: "Yeah! Oh, I won't give up. But I guess that's why I'm so discouraged."

Active listening is effective in getting teenagers to talk because each response by the counselor encourages the teenager to continue. The feedback the counselor gives the adolescent is verified as correct or incorrect, and in providing this verification, the counselee elaborates a little bit more. Slowly but surely a young person reveals his thoughts and feelings to the counselor.

At any point, the adult who evaluates a response, gives an opinion, suggests a solution, or has another agenda risks the teenager closing the door. As long as the counselor keeps focused on the teen's thoughts and feelings, and provides feedback that lets the adolescent know he's being heard and continually accepted unconditionally, the door remains open.

Naturally, there will come a time in the counseling process when other strategies are used in order to assist the young person in resolving conflicts, developing a strong identity, and taking responsibility for himself. Listening comes first, however. To understand a teenager accurately enables the counselor to be on track in his or her work. And, perhaps more importantly, when counselors listen to teenagers, the teenagers are much more willing to listen to counselors.

Getting teenagers to talk is indeed a challenge. It is worth all our efforts. To be a part of an adolescent's growth and development is one of the "highs" of a counselor's life. After all, it's what counselors are all about!

Seven

COUNSELING
STRATEGIES AND
TECHNIQUES

The idea is simple but profound: Effective counselors have a clear picture of the counseling process. They realize it begins with solid knowledge of adolescent growth and development. They realize that young people are trying to develop strong identities, an awareness of personal strengths and limitations, the ability to assert beliefs and feelings, the willingness to accept responsibility for their own actions, the competence to make informed decisions, the ability to relate to others and resolve conflict maturely, the skills necessary to be productive citizens, and a personal faith in God.

Counselors do not set these tasks for teenagers. They have been identified as the "work" adolescents must accomplish in order to prepare for the requirements of early adulthood. Effective counselors know, however, that they can create an environment and relationship that facilitate the growth and development of teenagers.

It is to this end that counselors help to create a therapeutic relationship in which teenagers allow them to be involved in their growth process. This relationship is built over time, using the various inter-action modes, qualities of effective helpers, and approaches that en-courage them to talk, all of which have been discussed earlier.

Next, the counselor helps teenagers explore and define "the prob-lem," and together they determine the goals of their work in coun-seling. For example, a young teenage girl tells you about a party she attended on the weekend. She is opposed to using drugs and is afraid of their negative and potentially deadly effects. In spite of her feel-ings about drugs, she could not refuse them when pressured by her friends at the party.

Your task as her counselor would be to help her define the prob-lem clearly and, if she is willing, determine and agree on a counseling goal. Notice that she does not appear ambivalent regarding her view of drugs — on this point she appears to have clarity. She has a strong conviction against the use of drugs. Her problem is learning to assert her conviction, preferably in a way that commands the respect of her friends, and standing firm, even if they don't. This focus helps her see the parameters of the problem and helps set the direction of the counseling process.

As her counselor you might say, "What would you think of our working on this together? You seem very clear and strong about your view of drugs. You don't want to use them. But you get lost when you're under pressure by your friends. Maybe we can find a way for you to get in touch with your strength when you are being pres-sured, and help you to say no in such a way that you don't jeopardize your friendships." If she agrees, the goal of counseling has been set.

It is at this point that the counselor has some work to do prior to helping a teenager reach a goal. The counselor needs to determine and select **strategies** that are likely to be most effective in assisting a teenager to reach a counseling goal. The consideration of appropri-ate strategies may take a few minutes or several days. Such consid-eration may include input from the counselee, resource people in the community, or other counselors. Some strategies might even take the approval or financial support of a teen's parents. In the end, however, the counselor chooses those strategies that he or she deems most effective.

In the previous example of the young girl, there are several strate-gies that might be considered. For example, as her counselor you might decide to have her read a book with which you are familiar that speaks about the concept of assertiveness. Or, you might want her to enroll in a six-week course on assertiveness training. Maybe you will want to provide her with several sessions of individual counseling before you place her in a group counseling experience led by a trained professional where she can practice her newly acquired as-sertion skills with other teenagers. It might be best to select and combine a variety of strategies. If you were a professional counselor, your selected strategies would comprise your **treatment plan.**

When the strategy selected is to provide personal counseling to the teen, various **techniques** can be used by the counselor to facilitate progress toward the counseling goal. Effective counselors are aware of the various techniques, and they use them all, as appropriate, in order to assist teens in their growth process. With the implementation of selected strategies and the use of various counseling techniques during the counseling process, the work of counseling is in full progress.

Together, the counselor and counselee make every effort to reach the goals of counseling. Sometimes, during the course of their work together, a counselor and counselee will find it necessary to reformulate the problem and/or goal. When this reformulation is completed, the work begins again. Finally, when the goals of counseling have been met, the counselor and counselee's work together ends. A few weeks later, and perhaps for a few months thereafter, it is advisable for the counselor and teenager to "touch base" to make sure that progress is continuing in a satisfactory manner.

Counseling professionals have a specialized vocabulary for these various steps in the counseling process. It is a more clinical language than the lay counselor uses, but it is descriptive of what is occurring between a counselor and counselee, client or patient. A **therapeutic alliance** is created, a **diagnosis** is determined, a **treatment plan** is developed and implemented, the counseling relationship reaches **termination** when the goals of the plan have been accomplished, and a **follow-up** is scheduled.

Lay counselors generally follow this same outline. The essential difference is that lay counselors work with teenagers who are within the normal range of growth and development, and refer more troubled teenagers who display signs of **psychopathology** to a trained professional.

Knowing these steps of the counseling process will enable the lay counselor to have a clear direction when working with teenagers. Once again, the clarity a counselor has about the counseling process is directly related to his or her counseling effectiveness. This clarity is what gives counseling its power as a constructive format to bring about the resolution of conflicts, the reaching of goals, and the stretching toward growth.

Counseling Techniques
The qualities of an effective helper are those personal characteristics which the counselor brings to a counseling relationship. They help to define who a counselor *is*. Strategies are general, overall plans which address a teenager's problem for the purpose of bringing resolution.

They describe the *direction* of the counseling process.

In contrast, techniques are methods, typically specific behaviors, which are implemented by a counselor to facilitate movement or growth by the teenager. Techniques are what the counselor *does* in a counseling session. "Methods" courses in college are those in which a student learns a variety of specific techniques which have been found to meet a goal. Counseling techniques are defined as the methods used by a counselor to help someone reach a counseling goal.

Certainly there are some activities that are implemented outside a session and away from a counselor's direct participation. These activities, however, are done by the counselee, not the counselor. For example, a counselor may give a teenager a "homework" assignment, whereby a teen who is working on the development of social skills may be asked to speak to three new people at school during the week. Perhaps the teenager is asked by the counselor to talk with a minister about an area of faith that is confusing and to report the results at the next counseling session. Such activities can be helpful in moving a teenager toward social or spiritual maturity.

Counselors cannot do the growing for teenagers. What they can do is implement certain techniques in a counseling session which have been found to facilitate a teenager's growth and development. The youth worker who plans to counsel teenagers will want to be aware of and be able to use a variety of these techniques.

There are, of course, specific techniques that are linked to contemporary counseling and therapy models and require specialized, graduate-level training. These techniques are for the purpose of helping bring about significant personality change or relief from emotional disorders. There are other techniques, however, that are appropriate for the lay counselor who is working with teenagers who are, for the most part, in the normal range of growth and development. These methods are effective tools for lay and professional counselors alike.

The Importance of Listening

The selection of a particular counseling technique is based on the counselor's ability to listen. Active listening, as described earlier, is that process that enables the counselor to know what the teenager is thinking and feeling at the moment. Along with the observation of a teenager's behavior and presentation, it is the listening process that determines the immediate selection and implementation of a counseling technique.

Listening is viewed by many as the foundation of all that follows in a counseling session. In fact, counseling of teenagers by lay counselors is the type of counseling professionals call **talk therapy.** One person talks, and the other one listens. Keith Olson, in his book *Counseling Teenagers,* says, "Without accurate listening the counselor is rendered totally ineffective. Listening is not so much a technique that the counselor uses or does as it is a required ingredient for all counseling."

The Question

Without a doubt, **questioning** is the most used technique of lay counselors. In fact, most counseling sessions probably begin with a question. "How are you today?" "What brought you to my office?" "How's it going?" A question begs for an answer. It is a stimulus to get someone else to respond. It gets things moving. The counselor is attempting to understand the teenager, but it is the teenager who embodies thoughts, feelings, behavior, experience, insight, and perceptions that are either a part of the problem or the solution.

Roger MacKinnon and Robert Michels wrote in their book, *The Psychiatric Interview in Clinical Practice,* "The psychiatrist demonstrates his expertise by the questions he both asks and does not ask." Whereas other mental health professionals may label their time with a client as a "session," psychiatrists and many psychologists call their interaction an **interview.** Such a term does not mean to infer that a counseling session is merely a question-and-answer format. It does suggest, however, that the technique of questioning is an effective and integral part of understanding a counselee.

A typical counseling session with a teenager using the technique of questioning might begin like this:

Counselor: "Hi, Mike. How are you doing today?"

Teenager: "Lousy. Nothing's going right."

Counselor: "What seems to be the problem?"

Teenager: "I'm failing a couple of classes, and my parents are going to jump all over me."

Counselor: "What do you mean?"

Teenager: "They're going to take my car away since my grades aren't good enough for them."

Counselor: "Did you know that before you got the bad grades?"

Teenager: "Oh, yeah. I really need my car, though."

Counselor: "What happened?"

Teenager: "I just don't seem to have enough time to study."

Counselor: "Do you really not have enough time?"

Teenager: "Oh, probably. I'm just not a very organized person. What do you think I should do?"

As the questions are asked, this teenager lets out more and more information. Most adults working with teens recognize the fact that few adolescents tell their whole story voluntarily. They are *willing* to do so, however, as long as the questioner appears sincere and nonjudgmental. But the story comes out in fragments. The patient listener hears what he needs to hear.

The counselor in this scenario has learned how Mike is feeling (lousy), why he is feeling bad (loss of car), and what Mike perceives to be his problem (disorganization). Also, the counselor has earned the right to be heard since he listened carefully to this teenager. In the end, Mike asks the counselor for help.

Here are some guidelines for the use of questioning as a technique which are important to keep in mind.

1. *Choose the technique of questioning with care.* The act of questioning another determines the direction of a counseling session. The questioner assumes that the line of questioning in progress is the significant material to be explored or discussed by the counselee. Nothing is more discouraging to a counselor than to spend a good deal of time questioning a teenager, only to have the adolescent say, "I know our time is almost up. But what I really wanted to talk to you about was. . . ." Suddenly you realize that you were working on *your* agenda, unaware of the teenager's need.

2. *Ask questions that relate to the teenager's counseling goal.* Teenagers are action-oriented people, and the act of counseling is rarely comfortable for long. Counselors learn quickly that their time with teenagers in a counseling setting is limited. Teenagers won't stay long. They have agreed to work on a specific goal; they aren't in our offices for a friendly chat. Asking questions that are related to the counseling goal is an efficient use of limited time. Such questions also help the teenager to stay focused on the issues at hand.

3. *Use open-ended questions with teenagers.* Teenagers will often use one-word answers. As counselors, however, we need more information if we are going to be helpful. For example, use "How do you feel about your mother?" rather than "Are you angry at your mother?" The first question gives the teenager much more latitude in exploring how he feels. The latter question only requires him to think about whether he is angry. The counselor is likely to get a yes or no answer.

Learning to ask timely, relevant, substantive, open-ended questions takes time. Professional counselors spend years refining this technique. The youth worker who counsels teens will be well-rewarded by becoming proficient in the use of the questioning technique.

The Probe

A second counseling technique is known as **probing.** A probe is a question that encourages the teenager to explore an area of concern more deeply. For example, a teenager may say he is depressed when asked how he feels. A probe would nudge this young man further:

"Do you have any idea why you feel depressed?" The probe enables the counselor to more fully understand what he is experiencing, and it provides the teenager with self-insight as well.

Additionally, the probe seeks to get a teenager to look at something that he has previously denied or resisted, an uncomfortable area to explore that the teenager would not examine without some help from the counselor. Let's look at an example of a probe.

A teenage boy has had several sessions with his counselor. Each time he has spent a significant amount of time blaming his recent girlfriend for their breakup. Once again, he begins to complain about this girl to his counselor.

> *Teenager:* "She's such a jerk! She was terrible. She has no respect for anybody."
>
> *Counselor:* "You really get upset when you think about her."
>
> *Teenager:* "Upset isn't the word for it. I get ANGRY! From the very beginning, she was always putting me down. And, she'd do it in front of my friends."
>
> *Counselor:* "She embarrassed you."
>
> *Teenager:* "I hope I never see her again."
>
> *Counselor: "If she was a jerk from the very beginning, why do you think you chose to spend time with her?"*
>
> *Teenager:* "Choose? What do you mean? She wanted to go with me."

Here we have the probe. It has not crossed this young man's conscious mind that he may have had something to do with choosing and staying in this relationship. The counselor's probe is in the form of a question. "Why do you think you chose to spend time with her?" The probe forces the young man to look at an idea that he has denied or resisted. If fact, his immediate answer suggests that he doesn't want to even consider such a thought. So he blames her for the decision to be in a relationship with her.

This probe, however, may be an important catalyst for his growth. He needs to understand why he was willing to stay in a destructive relationship for so long. It may not be enough for him to simply blame his ex-girlfriend, because if he gets involved with another person who abuses him, he will not have learned from his current experience. The probe, then, is an important technique for bringing to the conscious level a behavior pattern, an attitude, a belief, or a feeling that blocks normal growth and development. If and when the young man chooses to do something about his behavior, he need no longer feel like a victim.

A few guidelines need to be considered when using the technique of probing.

  1. *A therapeutic alliance needs to have been established before using a probe with a teenager.* By its very nature, a probe forces an

adolescent to look at an area that brings discomfort and anxiety. Keeping a teenager in therapy long enough to reach a counseling goal is difficult enough when the teen is comfortable. If the young person is not absolutely sure that you are on his side, premature termination of counseling is often the result. The timing of a probe is therefore crucial.

2. *The teenager's ego strength needs to be intact.* An adolescent may feel secure in the counseling relationship, but simply not be strong enough to confront an area of vulnerability. The last thing a counselor wants to do is frighten a teenager away at the very moment help is needed and wanted. Choose a time when you judge that the teenager is strong enough to consider the content of the probe. If you misjudge, simply back off and wait for a better time. A counselor's patience is generally rewarded.

3. *Allow a teenager to resist a probe.* The counselor's goal is not to prove a point. The idea is to sensitively encourage a young person to explore more deeply an area of experience that may lead to self-understanding and insight. A teenager's initial response is not necessarily the final response. Allowing teenagers to resist a probe may actually make it easier for them to consider the probe's content.

By its very nature, the probe nudges a teenager into unfamiliar territory. As a technique it serves the purpose of counseling very well. Its sensitive use, implemented in a timely manner, can serve as the catalyst for a teenager's growth.

The Reflection

Another useful counseling technique is **reflection.** This technique enables a counselor to reflect back to a teenager what the counselor has just heard the teenager say. Standing in front of a mirror serves a similar purpose. The images projected onto a mirror are reflected back to the person in front of the mirror. In the case of a mirror, people can see themselves as they appear to others.

In the counseling process, the purpose of reflection is twofold. First, reflection helps counselors to know whether or not they are hearing the counselee accurately. It is extremely important to hear what is being said from the teenager's point of view. Communicating this point of view back to the teenager allows the teenager to confirm, correct, or reject what the counselor has heard. As long as the counselor is tracking accurately, the process continues forward. However, counselors must make midcourse adjustments if the teenager corrects or rejects the "playback."

Let's look at the process of reflection through a couple of examples. An adolescent girl is in a counseling session with her counselor. Their dialogue is as follows:

Teenager: "I really want to go to the prom, but Tom hasn't asked me yet. All my friends are going. I can't figure out why he hasn't asked me."

Counselor: "You're afraid you'll be the only one not going if he doesn't call soon."

Teenager: "I'd be so embarrassed. People are already asking who I'm going with. I don't know what to tell them."

Counselor: "You're afraid of what people might think."

Teenager: "Right! They're going to think no one likes me."

At this time, this counselor's reflections are being confirmed as accurate. This young adolescent appears to be very concerned about being the only one in her peer group not attending the prom.

Now, let's change the dialogue in such a way that we can see how reflection works if the counselor is tracking inaccurately.

Teenager: "I really want to go to the prom, but Tom hasn't asked me yet. All my friends are going. I can't figure out why he hasn't asked me."

Counselor: "You're afraid you'll be the only one not going if he doesn't call soon."

Teenager: "Not really. Tom is a really neat guy, and I'm afraid he won't ask me."

Counselor: "Your relationship with Tom is pretty important to you."

Teenager: "Oh, yes! He's great! We've dated a couple of times, and I was hoping he'd ask me to the prom."

Counselor: "His taking you to the prom would indicate to you that your relationship with him is something special."

Teenager: "Exactly! Oh, I hope he calls me tonight!"

Through the use of reflection, this young girl's counselor learned quickly the girl's point of view. The counselor had initially focused on the teen's statement, "All my friends are going." Such a statement might suggest that this adolescent's concern centered on being the only person in her peer group staying home from the dance. The girl's response to the counselor's reflection, however, clearly let her counselor know that her concern focused on her fear that Tom might not like her as much as she had hoped. Her counselor quickly got back on track by stating, "Your relationship with Tom is pretty important to you." The counselee quickly confirmed this reflection as accurate.

The second purpose of reflection is for the benefit of teenagers. Reflections allow them to learn how others are viewing them. If what others are hearing or seeing is inaccurate, the teenagers are forced to be more precise in their presentation of themselves. And, perhaps more importantly, an accurate reflection by a counselor lets a teenager know that he is understood.

Here are a few guidelines to remember when using the technique of reflection.

1. *State a reflection in your own words.* Reflections are not simply verbatim repetitions of what the teenager has said. To repeat everything the teen says word for word would frustrate the young person. Can't you hear a teenager now? "What's the matter? Is something wrong with your hearing?" Effective reflections are the result of a counselor's accurate listening, maintaining the integrity of the teenager's point of view, and stating that point of view in the counselor's own words.

2. *Base your reflection on sufficient information.* Although one of the purposes of reflection is to allow for corrections, repeated inaccuracies may suggest to teenagers that a counselor is not listening or doesn't understand. Counselors will want teenagers to confirm their reflections most of the time. Basing reflections on sufficient information increases the chances of this occurring.

3. *Be careful not to overuse reflection.* Letting teenagers know their point of view is being heard is important. But excessive use of reflection can serve to interrupt the flow of thoughts and feelings of a teenager. Use reflection just often enough to let the teenager know you are accurately tracking and to assure yourself of the same.

In summary, the use of reflection is an effective technique for letting a teenager know he is being heard and understood, for assuring a counselor she is on track with a teenager's point of view, and for keeping the counseling process on course.

The Confrontation

Another technique counselors use is **confrontation**. As was just discussed, the technique of reflection is hearing the teen's point of view and communicating that *same* view back to the teenager. Confrontation, on the other hand, is for the purpose of encouraging the teenager to see a *different* view, a view he has never seen before, or a view that causes him some discomfort.

The technique is necessary due to the fact that teenagers are normally egocentric. In others words, they run all of their experience through their own grids, complete with their biases, inexperience, limitations, and goals.

Several years ago, as a high school counselor, I was talking to an eleventh-grade counselee of mine. I asked him how his career plans were going. "Great," he said. "I've decided to be a marine biologist." What I knew about this young man's academic record didn't bode well for a career in the sciences. He was friendly, energetic, and social. His grades in math and science courses, however, were not consistent with his career goal. In spite of this inconsistency, he saw himself as a marine biologist.

As his counselor, I had another view. I did not want to disappoint him, but I wanted him to recognize that whatever career he eventually chose, it would be important to him to have what it takes to succeed. Using the technique of confrontation, I said, "It's interesting that you have chosen a career in science when your grades suggest you might be much more successful in a nonscience field." He told me that he knew his math and science grades were low, but that he really wanted to be a marine biologist. I said to him, "I know you do. But in the long run, I don't know that you would be happy or successful as long as math and science are your weakest areas." Notice that the final decision was left to him.

The key to using confrontation with a counselee, particularly with teenagers, is the presence of an inconsistency. If I were to use one word to describe adolescents, it would be "inconsistent." Nowhere is this inconsistency more notable than in their social relationships.

Suppose a teenage girl is talking to her counselor about the fact that she can't seem to develop and maintain long-term relationships with her peers.

Teenager: "I expect my friends to be there for me when I need them. That's what friends are for."

Counselor: "Being there is important to you."

Teenager: "You got it! Just the other day, I needed to go shopping. I asked Judy to drive me to the shopping center because she has a car. She said she couldn't. *Wouldn't* is more like it! It was a Saturday."

Counselor: "Saturday was the only day you could go shopping."

Teenager: "No. But that's the best day for me."

Counselor: "So, Judy let you down, and you don't think she is much of a friend."

Teenager: "Can you believe it? I'm a better friend than that."

Counselor: "What was Judy's reason for not taking you?"

Teenager: "Oh, something about an algebra test on Monday. Said she had to study. I don't see why she couldn't have studied later. What's a friend for if you can't depend on her?"

Counselor: "Your friend is a good math student and didn't need to study all day."

Teenager: "Actually, she's doing real bad in that class. Her grade depends on the grade she got on that exam."

Counselor: *"You wanted Judy to take you shopping on a day that was convenient for you even though it might have jeopardized her grade in algebra?"*

Teenager: (Pause) "Well, yeah. I guess so." (She looks perplexed.)

Counselor: "I didn't hear you accurately."

Teenager: "That sounds pretty selfish."

Counselor: "You don't like the sound of it?"

Teenager: "No. I wouldn't want someone to ask me to do something if it might hurt me. Especially if it could be done at some other time. Boy, and I really told Judy off too."

This young girl was unaware of the inconsistency of her behavior. She thought her friend was thoughtless for not helping her get to the shopping center. Her counselor confronted her with the fact that she was seeing friendship as a one-way street. She was demanding, unreasonable, and self-centered in her attitude toward her friend.

The use of confrontation enabled this young adolescent to see herself as her friend experienced her. She could have argued with her counselor, denied her behavior, and resisted any need for change. Instead, she didn't like the sound of what she was hearing, and she didn't feel comfortable with the person she was seeing for the very first time: herself. She now had an opportunity to change the nature of how she related to others. This new view of herself may be just the information she needed to understand why she had so much trouble maintaining long-term relationships.

Consider these guidelines when using confrontation in counseling.

1. *Use confrontation when a therapeutic alliance has been established.* Confronting teenagers can be risky. Unless they are certain that you approach them with unconditional positive regard, they are likely to experience the confrontation as unsupportive of their personhood. They are more likely to consider the content of the confrontation if they know you are still there for them.

2. *Use a soft, supportive, matter-of-fact tone when confronting teenagers.* They need to hear another view as though it were an observation or a suggestion. If it feels judgmental, they are likely to defend their actions or withdraw from counseling.

3. *Give teens time to consider and integrate the content of a confrontation.* Remember that by nature they are egocentric, which is normal for their age-span. It will take longer for them to "see" another view than it might take for the normal adult.

The potential for bringing about change is great when confrontation is implemented with a counselee. Whenever teenagers (or adults, for that matter) see things differently, or become aware of something they hadn't seen before, or catch a vision of another way to do something, growth can occur.

The Interpretation

Another effective counseling technique is **interpretation.** Interpretation is used to explain the meaning of a person's belief system or behavior. Most people do not have a clear understanding of why they do what they do. Their thought processes and behavior patterns have evolved over time and any rationale for these processes and patterns has long since passed from memory, if a rationale ever existed consciously in the first place.

In the counseling process, a significant part of a counselee's work is trying to understand better the motivations and meanings of his behavior. Due to each individual's blind spots and emotional involvement, it is difficult, if not impossible, to "see the forest for the trees" without the objective help of another. A counselor, who is more objective, can see more readily the meanings of a counselee's behavior.

Other techniques such as questioning, probing, and reflecting are used much more often than interpreting. Interpretations can only take place when all of the component parts of an issue are present. A few years ago, a late adolescent came to a counselor's office because he seemed lost and directionless. He was having a difficult time describing himself apart from his parents, and he appeared to be delayed in his work of developing a clear sense of self-identity.

As time passed, he began to wonder about his growing interest in his biological parents. When his counselor remarked that she didn't know he had been adopted he said, "Oh, yes. Didn't I tell you that?" For the next few sessions, this young man began to express frustration about his interest in his real mother and father.

Teenager: "I don't know why I keep talking to you about my birth parents. I don't even know who they are. And, it would probably be impossible to find them."

Counselor: "You would like to know who your parents are but feel it's a waste of time."

Teenager: "Yeah, but I keep thinking about them and wondering where they are."

Counselor: "Do you think it would help if you found out who they are?"

Teenager: "I do. But, I don't know how it would help. I love my adoptive parents. After all, they have really been my Mom and Dad."

Counselor: "Perhaps finding out about your biological parents would help you figure out some of the questions you have about who you are. Not knowing them means you have gaps of information that make it more difficult to determine your identity."

Teenager: "You mean working on this identity stuff is related to my real parents?"

Counselor: "It's possible. What do you think?"

The counselor's interpretation could only be made following this teenager's disclosure of being adopted. Certainly adopted children have some questions that can only be answered by their biological parents. This counselor's interpretation not only gave this young man "permission" to continue talking about his biological parents, but it gave him insight into his sudden interest in wanting to know them.

There are times in counseling when teenagers reach a plateau. It's as though they can't find the next piece of the puzzle. An interpretation by a counselor can be the piece that nudges the teenager on. Movement begins again as the counselee and counselor work toward the completion of their agreed-upon goals.

Just as there are guidelines for using the previous techniques, the use of interpretation is most effective under the following conditions.

1. *Give an interpretation that is relevant to current issues being discussed.* Providing an explanation of a teenager's motivations is a "turn-off" unless it specifically relates to the problem at hand. In fact, doing so reminds teenagers of their parents. They will resist being "explained" by adults.

2. *Provide an interpretation when it appears the teenager needs one to continue moving forward.* The ideal situation is when a teenager arrives at the meaning of his behavior without being told by another. A counselor's timely interpretation, however, is far better than leaving the teenager blocked.

3. *Allow a teenager to resist an interpretation.* The mere fact that a teenager is considering the various motivations related to behavior is a positive direction. And, it's always possible that our interpretations are incorrect or incomplete. Remember that teenagers, at any given point, may not have disclosed all of the relevant information needed for a comprehensive and accurate interpretation.

The technique of interpretation can serve two very useful purposes. First, it can provide teenagers with new insight and understanding about their behavior; and second, it can help break logjams which stand in the way of growth.

Self-Disclosure

According to Sydney Jourard in his book, *The Transparent Self,* "Transparency begets transparency." Interestingly, he was writing to mental health professionals like himself. His point is that the disclosure of oneself as a counselor acts as encouragement to those with whom we work.

Self-disclosure in the clinical sense does not mean that counselors sit in counseling sessions talking about themselves to their counselees. Talking about past experiences, events, or situations does not necessarily indicate one is sharing the inner self with another. What self-disclosure does mean, however, is that counselors might consider sharing with their clients that which is occurring internally at that very moment as a result of the counseling relationship. In my book *Nothing to Hide,* I describe self-disclosure simply: "It is what is going on with me right at this moment as I respond and interact with you."

Suppose a teenager, filled with feelings of inadequacy, is embarrassed by her rapidly growing body. She is particularly concerned about the size of her feet.

Teenager: "I hate my feet. They're so ugly! In fact, they're bigger than all my friend's feet."

Counselor: "You've been looking at feet?"

Teenager: "At lunch today . . . we were all looking at each other's feet. And, mine were the ugliest. What if they just keep growing? I'm so embarrassed."

Counselor: "You're afraid everyone else thinks your feet are the ugliest too."

Teenager: "Of course! You wouldn't understand. You look great. You've probably always looked great."

Counselor: *"Actually, I was just remembering about my nose. When I was in high school, I was real self-conscious about my nose. I just knew everyone was looking at it."*

Teenager: "Really? You?"

Counselor: *"Yes, me. What I found out, though, was the rest of my face caught up with my nose. It's just that it grew first."*

Teenager: "Maybe that's how it will happen with me."

Counselor: "That's possible. Even if it isn't, though, you will probably not worry about it as an adult."

Teenager: "Thanks. I feel better."

In this example, the teenager's counselor identified as closely as possible with her experience. Such a disclosure can help this teenager worry less about and accept her changing body.

Self-disclosure can take on a different form, as well. A counselor might be working with a teenager who is extremely demanding and registers disappointment with just about everyone in her life. Her pattern is to withdraw when a friend or significant other fails to meet her expectations. This counselor begins to feel a sense of discomfort that gets in her way of listening to the adolescent. Finally the counselor says, "You know, it sounds as though everyone fails to meet your expectations sooner or later. You appear to handle these moments by terminating the relationship. I was sitting here thinking that, if that's the case, I will disappoint you eventually. Do you think you'll talk to me about it or leave counseling?"

This counselor has allowed what she is feeling inside to be expressed on the outside. The purpose of such self-disclosure is to encourage this teenager to explore her relationship patterns, including her expectations of others, and, if it would be helpful, to develop more constructive ways to handle her disappointment. That's what self-disclosure is all about.

Keep these guidelines in mind when using the technique of self-disclosure:

1. *Disclose what is going on at the moment as a result of the counseling relationship.* Self-disclosure is not meant to be a discussion of historical events. It is meant to give the teenager an idea of the impact he or she has on another person. In a way, the counselor is using the "self" as an instrument in the counseling process.

2. *Keep the focus of the self-disclosing statement on the teenager.* Any statement made by the counselor should be done because it has potential to assist the teenager to meet a counseling goal or to make progress toward healthy maturity. Self-disclosure should never be used to focus on self.

3. *Select self-disclosing statements that the teenager will be able to handle.* The counselor need not disclose everything in his or her life, but what is disclosed needs to be authentic. Use good judgment in what is shared with young people.

In summary, self-disclosure can encourage teenagers to share more openly. A counselor who is authentic and transparent in the counseling relationship is more likely to elicit from adolescents a similar response.

The Evaluative Statement

The use of an **evaluative statement** as a counseling technique might be confusing in light of the fact that unconditional positive regard has been previously indicated to be an important ingredient in the counseling process. It needs to be made clear, therefore, that evaluative statements are not used to make judgments of a counselee's personhood. For example, it isn't helpful to say to a teenager, "You seem to be pretty immature."

Nor should evaluative statements be used to compare one teenager with another. It will not facilitate the counseling process to say, "You are less mature than other teenagers in your youth group." Such statements say to the adolescent, "I don't like you." It isn't even helpful to make a positive comparison like, "You are smarter than your friends." Knowing you have made a positive comparison can indicate to a teenager that you can also make a negative comparison sometime in the future.

Evaluative statements can be useful, however, when they address a teenager's circumstances or behavior. Given the difficulty adolescents have in trying to communicate their feelings to their parents, it would be very helpful to say to a teen, "Your decision to share your feelings about your curfew with your parents should prove helpful in the long run." This is an evaluative statement that encourages mature behavior, particularly in the areas of conflict resolution and the assertion of feelings. The opposite evaluation could prove just as useful. "Your decision to withhold from your parents your feelings about your curfew may make it difficult for them to see your readiness for increased independence."

Evaluative statements enable counselors to share their judgment regarding a teenager's behavior. Although adolescents do think like adults (formal operations), they are not yet highly skilled in the evaluation process. They often are unaware of all the options. They are inexperienced, and they tend to be impulsive. The mature judgment of a counselor can help teenagers stop long enough to evaluate their actions until they have become more accomplished at this skill.

Since evaluative statements are either positive or negative judgments of a teenager's behavior, there are infinite opportunities to use this counseling technique. "Your drinking to feel better won't help you solve your problems." "Telling your girlfriend that you are not ready for a serious relationship will help her know she is still OK as a person." "You handled that situation in a very mature manner." "It took a lot of strength to admit you were wrong."

Be aware of the following guidelines when using evaluative statements as a counseling technique.

1. *Use evaluative statements in order to share your judgment of a teenager's behavior.* Such statements distinguish between the person and the person's behavior. It is never helpful to indicate to teenagers that they are "good" or "bad." Counselors must communicate their acceptance of the *person* as unconditional. Their judgment of a teenager's *behavior,* however, will vary.

2. *Use evaluation when it is apparent the teenager hasn't used judgment or is unable to do so.* Remember that mature judgment is not gained overnight. Teenagers need time and practice in using this skill. A mark of maturity is good judgment. In a way, counselors are sharing such judgment until teenagers are capable of making independent judgments of their own.

3. *Use evaluation to help guide teenagers to adult behavior.* It is not necessary to evaluate every behavior of a teenager. Select those moments in the counseling process in which the direction of a teenager's growth is likely to be facilitated or hindered by the way he or she acts.

Although evaluation should be used sparingly, it can be a helpful guide for teenagers who are trying to find their way. Teenagers are not given the luxury of learning adult skills before they are required to use them. A counselor's judgment regarding a teenager's progress can be very reassuring to the teen.

Teaching, Affirmation, and Silence

These behaviors have been placed together, not because they are similar, but because they have already been mentioned. They are facilitative behaviors, however, and are considered to be counseling techniques.

Teaching is that process whereby we provide teenagers with information they need to know in order to facilitate their growth and development. Counselors generally use discretion when teaching because it is preferable in counseling to enable teenagers to discover important information on their own.

There are times, however, when information is needed at a particular moment in a counseling session in order to continue exploring an issue. There are other times when information that would be helpful is not readily available or easily obtained. The time and investment necessary for the teenager to obtain the information does not justify having to delay the counseling process. It is at these times that a counselor will impart information in order to enable the teenager to continue the informed exploration of issues.

Since it was originally mentioned that teaching is a different interaction mode than counseling, it might be useful to distinguish between teaching as a role and teaching as a technique. Most teachers do some counseling and most counselors do some teaching. If I am assigned or assume the role of counselor, my *primary* function is to counsel. As a counselor, I may periodically choose the technique of teaching in order to impart important information, but teaching is only one of several techniques I use. And, although I am using the technique of teaching, I do not shed my role as a counselor.

Affirmation occurs throughout the counseling process. The whole idea of expressing empathy, unconditional positive regard, and acceptance of the teenager's point of view is that of affirming the value and worth of a young person. Even though affirmation is inherent to counseling, it should be remembered that teenagers respond to affirming words.

Youth Specialties, a Christian organization that provides youth workers and parents with resources for working with teenagers, likes to call language that affirms teenagers "Way to Go!" phrases. They suggest using phrases like: "You handled that situation well"; "It sounds like you really care about your friends"; "Good thinking!"; "How thoughtful"; "I know you can do it"; and "I really appreciate you."

While these "Way to go" phrases are direct, affirmative statements, Youth Specialties also suggests some phrases in which the value and worth placed in a teenager is inherent in the wording. These include: "What's your opinion?"; "Will you pray for me?"; and "What do you think you can do to change it?" When teens are treated as having value and worth, they tend to give you their best thinking on a matter.

Silence was described earlier as a passive listening approach. Naturally, there are times when counselors need to be actively listening in order to insure that a teenager's point of view is being heard accurately. There are other times, however, when we know the young person's point of view, and he or she knows we know! This is the time to consider using the technique of silence. This is particularly true when we know that the teenager is working on the issues at hand.

Silence says much to the teenager. "I'm listening, go on." "You're doing fine." "What you have to say is important." "I have every confidence in your ability to work through this." "I don't need to control the agenda." "The responsibility for your growth belongs to you." In a way, silence is a form of affirmation.

Silence allows a teenager to process issues without being distracted or interrupted by another's voice. By being silent, the counselor enables the adolescent to spontaneously express thoughts, feelings, perceptions, insights, values, fears, and possible solutions as they rise to the counselee's conscious mind. The counselor can register all that is being said, reserving comment for a later time. The important thing when a counselee is working is to allow her to work! After all, this is the goal of counseling.

A Final Word

It might be easy for a relatively new lay counselor to feel inadequate to the task of implementing the various elements of the counseling process, including the techniques described in this chapter. It can't be denied that much is going on in counseling teenagers. The counselor must develop a therapeutic relationship, help to define the teenager's problem, assist in setting counseling goals, determine strategy, implement techniques, terminate the counseling relationship, and provide for follow-up. The task is challenging!

Before anyone is frightened away, however, remember that professional counselors refine their craft over a period of *several years!* No one expects the new counselor to know all there is to know or be completely proficient when he or she begins counseling teenagers.

As a lay counselor, you will want to read and learn all you can about normal adolescent behavior and the developmental tasks of this age-span. Become familiar with the various strategies and techniques that facilitate growth and development. Find a professional counselor with a Christian perspective who can provide you with support and counsel and to whom you can refer troubled youth. As you help teenagers in the counseling sessions, you will become a more accomplished counselor.

Eight

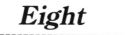

THE CHALLENGE OF COUNSELING TEENAGERS

Many mental health professionals believe it is more difficult to establish a counseling relationship with teenagers than it is with children or adults. Although there are exceptions, it is likely that most children are *brought* to the counselor by their parents, and adults *choose* to seek counseling more often than not. Adolescents, however, are typically *sent* to a counselor's office. Naturally, counseling is more productive when the counselee comes to a counselor on a voluntary basis. Therefore, before a therapeutic relationship can be established with a teenager, this enormous obstacle must be hurdled.

There are other challenges as well—developmental, legal, and ethical issues. Effective counselors are aware of these issues and have some strategies in mind for dealing with them as they are presented.

The Need to Separate
The first challenge in counseling teenagers is developmental. As has been noted previously, adolescents have a major developmental task:

to determine identity apart from parents. This appears, on the surface, to be an ideal area in which counselors can provide assistance. Together, it would seem, the counselor and teen can explore, understand, and complete all of the nuances of becoming an adult.

Ironically, the challenge of counseling resides at the very core of this teenage task! In order to determine identity, teenagers must experience a **separation** from their parents and other significant adults. Distance is essential in order for them to formulate their own thoughts, feelings, behavior patterns, plans, relationships, values, and priorities. Adults often overwhelm these vulnerable "adults-in-the-making" because their identities are so strong in comparison to these emerging adults. So teens go into hiding from these well-meaning people in their lives.

At the very time that these young people are becoming quite skilled in a variety of defensive maneuvers, they are sent to a professional counselor. (Or, in the case of a lay counselor, a teenager's parents have requested that a youth leader talk to their son or daughter.) Regardless of the fact that counselors are not attempting to serve as surrogate parents, adolescents often assume they are.

Most people, including teenagers, behave in the counselor's office about the same way they act in the world-at-large. In other words, counselors are not immune to the defensive stance of teenagers.

The adolescent needs space and distance and the counselor is inviting openness and intimacy. Teenagers are saying to adults, "Leave me alone. I need to figure out things on my own." Counselors are saying, "Talk to me. Open up. Maybe I can help." The challenge is clear: *The teen's need is for distance, and a counselor is calling for closeness!* In a way, the counseling process is out of sync with the developmental process.

Ignoring this challenge is foolish, and ordering teenagers to talk openly is futile. How can the lay counselor deal with such an intricate problem? Keeping the following principles in mind will help you deal with this challenge.

1. The developmental task of teenagers to separate and develop identity is a healthy process.
2. In spite of all of your good intentions and ability to help, you will not be able to counsel every teenager you face.
3. The various strategies and techniques used by counselors have been time-tested. Trust them. They are the most effective techniques we have developed to date.
4. Teenagers make the decision to participate fully in the counseling process. Counselors cannot make this decision for them.
5. Personalizing a teenager's decision to refuse counseling is neither useful nor necessary. A teenager's decision has more to do with personal issues than it has to do with the counselor.

6. If parents requested counseling for their teenager, encourage them when the teenager decides not to participate in the process. Let them know that they demonstrated their care and acted responsibly.
7. A teenager may decide later to get involved in the counseling process with you. Be open to that fact. Seize the day!

Counselors cannot alter the pattern of development but must work within its parameters.

The Teenager's View of the Counselor

The process of **transference** is another challenge to counseling teenagers. It is a process whereby a teenager unconsciously and inappropriately displaces onto the counselor those behavior patterns and emotional reactions that are expressive of his relationship with significant others. For example, a teenager may respond to a counselor as though he were responding to his parents.

Transference can be positive or negative. For example, a teenage boy might try to please the counselor, a response which is similar to his interaction pattern with his father. On the other hand, a counselor might have a teenager who displays negative transference. Suppose a teenager has an extremely alienated relationship with her father, and her counselor is a male. She begins to unconsciously and inappropriately respond toward her counselor with anger and hostility, and she becomes argumentative and abusive. Unless the counselor recognizes her behavior as negative transference, this teen's response patterns will be very confusing to him. Note that both positive and negative transference are seen as unconscious and inappropriate attitudes and behavior which are "transferred" to the counselor.

Perhaps the most common form of transference a lay counselor will experience is being treated like a surrogate parent. When parents exercise their authority over their young children, there is a large "control" component. Peter Buntman and E.M. Saris address this point in their book *How to Live with Your Teenager*. "When children are small we use both our authority and our control—our authority when we influence behavior and our control in areas affecting our children's health, safety, and welfare."

Parents tend to continue their authority/control stance even when their children become teenagers. Adolescents, of course, want to control their own lives and make their own decisions. They generally resist being told what to do by others, particularly adults. It is at this juncture that teenagers may transfer their attitudes and feelings toward their parents to the counselor, reasoning that the counselor is another adult trying to tell them what to do.

In a way, the counselor has an opportunity to model a new relationship that teens can have with adults. The counselor *is* an authority figure. However, this "authority" is not of the control variety. Instead it is more influential. Buntman and Saris suggest this approach to parents of teenagers. "As our children grow older and bigger, control needs to be lessened. You need to use more authority/influence. You need to trust that your teen can learn to make his own decisions—whether they are right or wrong." Counselors understand this type of relationship.

There are some counseling approaches, particularly psychoanalytic theory, that use transference as an integral part of the treatment process. This is beyond the scope of lay counselors working with relatively healthy adolescents. What is appropriate, however, is to listen to the positive and negative attitudes and feelings being expressed through transference, and use the counseling technique of interpretation to help the teenager understand and resolve them.

Interestingly, counselors sometimes unconsciously and inappropriately displace on teenagers behavior patterns and emotional reactions that are expressive of their relationships with significant others. This is known as **countertransference.** For example, a counselor may begin to respond to a teenager in counseling as though the teenager were his or her child. Counselors need to be aware of their own countertransference so that their feelings and attitudes do not inhibit the counseling process. Such feelings need not and should not be expressed to the counselee.

Consider the following guidelines when dealing with transference.

1. *Educate teenagers regarding your role.* Answer any questions they have regarding what you do and counseling in general.
2. *Treat teenagers as you would another adult.* Allow them to make decisions whenever possible. Steer clear of language that elicits guilt, serves to intimidate, or is manipulative. Be influential rather than controlling.
3. *Interpret their feelings and attitudes about you.* Remember that their displacement of feelings toward you is not conscious or deliberate. Do not correct their behavior for being inappropriate.
4. *Be aware of your own countertransference issues.* Counselors are human and have feelings too. Sometimes in the course of therapy with a teenager, you will tap into your own conflicts.

The Minor Status of Teenagers

The fact that most of the teenagers lay counselors counsel will be younger than eighteen presents a legal challenge to counseling. Teenagers may *want* to be adults, but the fact is they hold minor status in our society. They are not legal adults until they reach the age of eighteen; and even those who have reached eighteen may not yet have become independent, especially in a financial sense. Teenagers typically come to counseling dependent on their parents.

Complication comes from the fact that parents are the *responsible party* for minors. What teenagers decide in a counseling session may need the approval or at least the support of their parents. Some parents are more interested and involved in the counseling process than others, but the point is that teenagers do not enter counseling entirely independent.

The difficulty becomes clear. Counselors are often helping teenagers develop an identity apart from their parents at the same time that their parents are vitally interested in the outcome of the counseling process! The counselor has to walk the narrow line between encouraging teenagers to work toward independence and assuring parents that they need not be intimately involved in the counseling process in order for the outcome to be healthy and beneficial.

Most caring parents are very interested in the content and process of their children's counseling. They typically would like to know what is talked about even though they intuitively know that such knowledge may very well impede their children from sharing what they are thinking and feeling with their counselor. As counselors, we must empathize with parents who feel helpless in the process.

The problem is further complicated by the fact that many parents don't fully understand the purpose and process of counseling. In fact, a significant number of parents probably share the same view of counseling as their children: Counselors are surrogate parents. If their children are not developing in the manner desired, they send them to a counselor in order to get them back on track. It's a perception of counseling that suggests that the parents determine the agenda for counseling, and the counselor implements it.

This is not to suggest that a counselor's work with a teenager is inconsistent with a parent's agenda. In truth, both counselors and parents desire that the counseling process will serve to help and encourage a teenager to grow toward mature adulthood. But parents continue to want to be involved in the direction of their teenagers' growth, similar to their involvement when their children were smaller and younger.

Most parents are very responsible people. Many feel they have not met the requirements of parenting until their kids "have their act together." The wise counselor knows, however, that teenagers may never *need* to have their act together as long as their parents remain responsible for them. *Teenagers need to separate from their parents, and parents need to let go of their teenagers.*

Counselors must work with parents in such a way that the parents feel valued and respected. These parents have a right to know the nature and direction of your work with their children, but they also need to know that they must trust you as their son or daughter's counselor in order not to impede the counseling process. Teenagers will discontinue talking to a counselor if they think their counselor is "reporting" the contents of a session back to their parents.

Working with teenagers and parents is a unique challenge in counseling adolescents. Counselors must have parental support in order to counsel minors. On the other hand, these parents must accept the fact that they must give up some control of the process in order for counseling to be successful.

Consider the following ideas when working with teenagers and their parents.

1. Educate parents regarding the purpose and process of counseling. They have a right to know since they are responsible for their children.

2. Let teenagers know that their parents have a right to know the content and process of all counseling sessions. Also tell them that you do not anticipate "reporting" your sessions to parents *unless you determine that it is in the teenager's interest and welfare to do so.* Such a stance may mean that a teenager is less likely to tell you something of importance, but it is generally better to leave yourself the freedom to talk to parents when it is critically important. As trust is built, teenagers typically will share what they need to share even though you may report it to their parents.

3. Before reporting any information from a session to a teenager's parents, notify the teenager in advance and give your rationale for doing so. Nothing turns a teenager off more quickly than talking about a session behind his or her back. It saves a lot of grief to be open and direct about your intentions.

4. Discuss with parents the fact that they have a right to know what is occurring in a counseling session with their child. Also tell them that reporting details of each session will impede any progress. Try to get them to agree to your sharing only material that you determine is critical for them to know. Assure them that you will let them know anything that concerns their teenager's health, safety, or welfare.

5. Meet with a teenager's parents periodically to get their input and evaluation of their child's progress. They need to be involved in a limited but significant way as you work with their teenager.

Confidentiality and Duty to Report
Counselors can be faced with a complex dilemma if they disclose to others information gained during the course of counseling. Counselors want to provide an atmosphere which encourages teenagers to discuss fully the current and relevant issues of their lives. During

counseling, however, the counselor may hear information that suggests the teenager may be in danger, (i.e., possible suicide, sexual abuse), or that his or her behavior may threaten someone else (i.e., possible commitment of a crime).

What information should be disclosed to others? Why is this question a complex issue? Disclosing information may be in the best interest of the teenager, but disclosing information that has been given to a counselor in confidence may limit the amount of information the teenager is willing to share in the future.

Privileged communication and confidentiality are two issues you, as a lay counselor, need to know about. The more you know about these issues, the more effective you will be in helping teenagers and reducing or preventing problems in the future.

Privileged communication is the legal right to prevent information gained in therapy to be used in a court of law. Interestingly, the **holder of the privilege** is the client rather than the therapist or counselor. In most cases where a teenager is the client, the parents are the holders of the privilege. Therefore, a mental health professional that is given psychotherapist-patient privilege by the laws of a state must receive permission from the client before disclosing such information to a court of law. *Lay counselors do not hold psychotherapist-patient privilege.* This means that information given to a lay counselor by a teenager can be subpoenaed by a court of law.

Confidentiality, by contrast, is an ethical issue rather than a legal requirement. It is a standard of professional conduct agreed on by members of the counseling profession regarding the disclosure of information. Confidentiality means that certified or licensed counselors do not reveal information regarding a client to another person without the express permission of the client. To do so is not illegal, but it is unethical and could lead to the loss of licensure.

In the case of adolescents, confidentiality rests with the parents. Professional counselors, with a few notable exceptions, must gain the permission of a teenager's parents before disclosing information to a third party.

Lay counselors are not bound by the ethical requirements of confidentiality because they are not considered members of the counseling profession and are not governed by the profession's Code of Ethics. In order to be so considered, an individual must be studying in an accredited counselor education program, working toward licensure, or counseling as a certified or licensed mental health professional. As we consider guidelines for lay counselors regarding these issues, however, there is much wisdom in the lay counselor adopting the same standards relating to confidentiality as those maintained by professional therapists.

There are specific exceptions to the legal and ethical requirements of privileged communication and confidentiality. These are the times when the information learned by the professional counselor results in a **duty to report.** Under ordinary circumstances, such reporting would be a breach of confidentiality and considered unethical. In a duty-to-report situation, however, there is no need for permission from the client or a teenager's parents.

The following is a list of duty-to-report situations.

1. Mental health professionals must take every precaution to prevent self-harm by a client. For example, a professional counselor who determines that there is a possibility of an attempted suicide by a client must disclose such information to appropriate personnel and agencies who are needed to stabilize the client.

2. Mental health professionals, among others, are required to report immediately any reasonable suspicion of child abuse or neglect to the appropriate child protective agency. Every state has legal requirements related to the reporting of child abuse, and professional counselors must be aware of the requirements in their state. Notice that these requirements do not imply that a counselor must inform the parents of the child.

3. In some states, mental health professionals have a duty to warn the potential victims of crimes that have been disclosed by a client during the course of counseling. Professional counselors must be aware of their state's requirements.

In each of these instances, there is a potentially life-threatening circumstance that takes precedence over the normal handling of information. Confidentiality is to be upheld except in those cases where there is a clear and imminent danger to the welfare of an adult client, a minor child, or others.

Child-care custodians are also required to report reasonable suspicion of child abuse or neglect. Employees of public and private schools, child-care or day-care centers, residential care facilities, and group homes, social workers, probation officers, and foster parents are examples of child-care custodians. These people are mentioned because individuals who work with children in their careers often volunteer to work with children during their leisure time. For example, a junior or senior high school teacher who volunteers to work with the teenagers at church is a child-care custodian. Teachers are required by law to report reasonable suspicion of child abuse. Individuals holding these types of positions should check the regulations of their state regarding the requirements of reporting.

Lay counselors who do not hold child-care positions are not *required* to report such cases but are *strongly encouraged* to do so. It makes sense for lay counselors to take whatever steps they deem necessary to help teenagers whose welfare appears to be in danger.

Although mental health professionals and child-care custodians usually must indicate their identities, lay men and women may make a report of child abuse anonymously. Lay counselors are encouraged to check the exact requirements for reporting in their state.

Although privileged communication and confidentiality issues are directed toward members of the counseling profession, they can serve to guide the lay counselor regarding the disclosure of information teenagers reveal in a counseling session. The following suggestions are made for the lay counselor.

1. *Inform the teenager with whom you are counseling of the limits of confidentiality.* Parents are legally the "holder of the privilege," and lay counselors do not have psychotherapist-patient privilege. It is generally agreed in the mental health field that clients have the right to know how information they share might be disclosed in the future. Even though it may inhibit the amount of information a teenager shares, most professional counselors believe it minimizes problems in the future.

2. *Tell teenagers with whom you are counseling how you plan to handle matters relating to their health, safety, and welfare.* You have told them that their parents have the legal right to know about their counseling, but also let them know about other people you might need to consult. For example, you might need to exchange information with a school counselor or medical doctor, provided that you have permission from the teenager's parents. They may not like what they hear, but they will respect your forthrightness.

3. *Be alert to the possibility of child abuse, neglect, or sexual abuse.* Learn the procedures for reporting such cases in your community. Voluntarily make a report if you have a reasonable suspicion of child abuse, neglect, or sexual abuse. You need not inform the parents if you deem it unwise. You may also remain anonymous.

4. *Take care that you do not casually or inadvertently reveal information about a teenager to anyone who does not have a legal right to know.* Disclosing personal information is not in the best interest of a teenager and may even be dangerous. Once teenagers learn that you talk about them outside of your counseling session, your counseling days with teens are over.

5. *Under nonemergency circumstances, obtain permission from a teenager's parents before disclosing any information.* Remember that they are the holder of the privilege for their minor-age children. It is usually best to get permission in writing.

6. *Know your own limits in training and experience as a lay counselor.* It is challenging enough for a counseling professional to accurately assess **suicidal ideation** and **suicidal intent.** If a

teenager threatens to hurt himself or someone else, do not hesitate to inform his parents or other appropriate authorities. It is better to make an error in judgment in favor of the teenager's welfare.

Careful consideration should be given before disclosing information about a teenager to a third party. This consideration should weigh the teenager's desire for privacy, the parents' legal right to information, the fact that confidentiality rests with parents, and the young person's welfare. Finding the appropriate balance is a challenging proposition. Every effort made to reach this balance will help facilitate an adolescent's growth and development, maintain a parent's cooperation and support, and assure the teenager's welfare.

Lack of Continuity

One final challenge to counseling teenagers is the difficulty of meeting on a regular, systematic, and comprehensive basis. Teenagers are busy people. They rarely sit around one place for long. They change their focus and priorities by the moment. Persistence, discipline, and follow-through are not their strong suits. Therefore, a lack of continuity is common in a counseling relationship.

The need for continuity is more important to a counselor than a teenager. Because this is true, counselors recognize that counseling is "done on the run" with teenagers. Counseling professionals, due to the pathology that might be present, can sometimes work with a teenager for a number of months up to a couple of years. A teenager who is clinically depressed, for example, is more likely to remain in counseling for a while.

Lay counselors working with teenagers within the normal range, however, rarely have the opportunity to systematically work with an individual for very long. The pattern of counseling is more fragmented—a couple of sessions here, a session there, and a break for several months. It may not be as efficient as we might wish, but the fact is that we must wait for teenagers to fit us into their busy schedules!

Patience is the key to working with teenagers. They may live in the "now," but effective counselors take a long view. Most youth workers have a three- or four-year opportunity to work with an individual teenager. The effective counselor sits back, develops healthy relationship patterns, gains a reputation of caring for kids, and seizes the opportunity to counsel with a teenager when it comes.

Counseling teenagers is a challenging task. At times it feels as though it will take a miracle to get into a position to counsel with a particular teenager. When you "hang in there," however, teenagers are likely to recognize you as an adult they can trust. When their need for help and your desire to assist merge, the resulting counseling relationship can facilitate growth and development.

Nine

WORKING WITH
THE TEENAGER'S
FAMILY

Historically, counseling has focused on working with the individual client. An individual experiencing problems and displaying dysfunctional behavior patterns would either seek or be sent for treatment. The client's problems were seen as emanating from within, which made the individual the proper focus for treatment.

Theories of counseling and a myriad of techniques appropriate to each theory were created and developed for implementation on an individual basis. Patricia Boyer and Ronald Jeffrey describe the consequence of seeing the individual as the sole patient in their book *A Guide for the Family Therapist.* "Minimal attention was given to the fact that a person's pain was both a cause and a product of psychological and emotional pain within the family or to the idea that actions and reactions of others close to a person might shape that person's behavior."

In the 1950s, a significant number of therapists working with schizophrenic children on an individual basis began to question the effectiveness of their approach. Bateson and others, writing for the professional journal *Behavioral Science,* described the fact that very little progress was being made with these children when they continued to live at home. Others noticed that children who improved with individual therapy on being institutionalized regressed when they returned home.

These pioneers of family counseling began to recognize that families represented a **system** that impacted and affected children who were a part of them. This recognition led to the family being accepted as the proper focus of treatment. L'abate, Ganahl, and Hansen, in their book *Methods of Family Therapy,* write, "Family therapy is generally based on the belief that a family is a system, and the therapeutic process involves treating the whole system or individuals and subsystems regarding their interaction with the whole system."

The Committee on Child Psychiatry provides a clear perspective of family counseling in its book *The Process of Child Therapy.* "The child who is referred because of symptomatic behavior reflects conflicting forces acting with the family, and these forces interfere with the growth and individualization of the various family members. Thus, the entire family is viewed as the patient."

Lay counselors recognize that much of their interaction will be with individual teenagers. They do not pretend to be counseling professionals, nor have they been given "permission" by parents to become the family's therapist. Understanding that each teenager is impacted by a family gives the youth worker an alternative to working with the individual adolescent. Periodically, counseling teenagers includes working with other members of the family as well.

Approaching Family Counseling

The developers and researchers of family counseling have conceptualized complex and sophisticated theories and techniques regarding family interaction patterns. All of them, however, relate in some way to the concept that the individual is a part of a larger whole. The teenager (a part) influences and is influenced by the family (the whole). In order to help a teenager, the counselor will have to determine the family's role in creating and maintaining dysfunction.

It is unlikely that the lay counselor will be involved with the intricate designs of these theoretical approaches because of the specialized training and expertise needed. Nevertheless, there will be many opportunities for a youth worker to counsel with entire families in a significant and helpful way.

The Problem-Solving Approach

Many lay counselors address family counseling with a *problem-solving approach.* This perspective gives the counselor a clear definition of role and goal. The *role* of the counselor is that of a problem-solver, and the *goal* is for families to develop healthy ways of interacting that facilitate growth and development of individual family members.

In their book *Systemic Family Therapy,* William Nichols and Craig Everett describe the counselor's role and purpose in family counseling. "The therapist approaches the family system as an outsider who has been asked in one way or another to intervene in the life of the family. . . . The therapist comes to the family with the task of assessing the family system and engaging the family in treatment for the purposes of alleviation and elimination of symptoms and making changes that will assist the family in achieving improvement in its ongoing functions."

In terms of the lay counselor who works with families within the normal range of development, the role and goal would be as follows: *The lay counselor helps the family to define its problems and engages the family in counseling for the purpose of assisting individual members to grow within the context of a healthy family climate.* Family counseling for this purpose can be initiated by any member of the family or by the counselor when it is recognized that the problems experienced by the teenager appear to be related to the entire family.

Boyer and Jeffrey theorize that most problems of families are centered on the following areas: (1) communication; (2) self-concept reinforcement; (3) family member expectations; (4) handling differences; and (5) family rules. They suggest that the manner in which families interact in these areas determines either a positive or negative climate. Obviously, the adult who works closely with teenagers and their families is in a good position to note any problem areas.

How would the problem-solving approach to family counseling work? Let's say that a youth worker notices that one of the teenagers in the youth group appears to have a very low level of confidence, even though she is attractive, intelligent, and well-liked by her peers. Realizing that the family is a major contributor to self-concept reinforcement, the youth worker suggests to her parents that the entire family might be needed to help this young lady feel better about herself. A meeting of the entire family is requested, and the parents agree.

During the meeting, this counselor observes the family's interaction patterns as she introduces herself to each member and learns something about each participant. She begins to be aware that "put-downs" of each other are regularly verbalized. The consequence of this behavior leads to defensiveness and counterattacks. And, the teenager whose self-concept and level of confidence are low begins to withdraw. As a problem-solver, this counselor helps this family see the destructive nature of "put-downs," and introduces them to the idea that families need to support the value and worth of each other. If the family agrees to work toward a more supportive atmosphere as a goal, this counselor will help them develop ways to increase the number of supportive messages being sent and received by family members.

Perhaps another counselor notices that a young teenage boy seems to be in a perpetual state of alienation with his parents. Recognizing that the handling of differences can be a major problem area for families, this youth worker sets up a meeting with the teenager's family. During the session, the counselor tries to find out how differences are handled in the family. What becomes apparent is that problems experienced by the family are routinely avoided. Members evidently do not discuss their disagreements or acknowledge them for fear they will become worse.

This lay counselor points out to the family that disagreements can be handled in a variety of ways. Boyer and Jeffrey, for example, suggest families handle disagreements either by attack, avoidance, surrender, or negotiation. The family in this example obviously uses avoidance as its method of handling differences. Avoidance worsens the problem because differences can never be resolved by acting as though they aren't there. The counselor in this case would try to get the family to agree to the goal of learning to solve its problems through the process of negotiation, and would then expend energy to implement this goal.

For purposes of clarity, I have called the above perspective the problem-solving approach. In the literature of family counseling, it is a simplification of the *strategic model* of family counseling. Jay Haley defined strategic therapy in his book *Uncommon Therapy* as follows: "Therapy can be called strategic if the clinician initiates what happens during therapy and designs a particular approach for each problem."

Haley later characterized strategic therapy in two ways: (1) It is a therapy approach in which the counselor actively intervenes to change behavior and relationship patterns, and (2) It is an approach that focuses on problem-solving and goal-oriented activities. Stephen Schultz defines strategic therapy as it relates to family counseling in a similar way in his book *Family Systems Therapy*. "The strategic therapist is a problem-definer whose job is to take the presenting complaint or symptom and frame a solvable problem. If the patient presents with a problem that can be solved as defined, then by all means go ahead and solve it. If not, then reframe it so that it can be solved."

What youth worker hasn't heard a teenager complaining about an unreasonable curfew? As a counselor, you may ask the teen, "Have you talked to your parents about how you feel?" Her reply is typical. "Are you kidding? My parents are too old to understand teenagers today." This teenager has "framed" the problem as one in which her parents are too old to ever know what modern teenagers need. It is an unsolvable problem because these parents cannot become younger.

In the problem-solving approach or strategic model, the counselor would "reframe" the problem. "It sounds like you haven't found a way to convince your parents that you can handle more responsibility because you are older." Now this teenager has a solvable problem. Her parents don't have to shed their years. She has to find a way to show them that she has grown in terms of being more responsible for her behavior. Having redefined the problem, the counselor may be able to work with the girl and her parents in negotiating a new curfew.

Implementing family counseling as a problem-solving approach can be an extremely effective method for helping teenagers. It is an approach that recognizes that teenagers do not live in a vacuum. They interact either positively or negatively with their families. The manner in which this occurs can be influenced by a counselor.

The Developmental Approach

A second approach to family counseling is based on a *developmental approach.* This perspective is based on the idea that families move through several identifiable, predictable stages, each requiring changes that permit growth and movement to the succeeding stage. Schultz defines this view in the following manner: "The developmental model rests upon the very simple notion of the family life cycle, the idea that over time the family's composition and the tasks facing it change in certain predictable ways. It is convenient to describe the life cycle as a series of stages of family development."

Families that have adolescent children present a most interesting stage of life. While adolescents are changing from children to adults, parents are finding it necessary to redefine their own lives. As the oldest child draws closer to adulthood, parents begin to realize that parenting will not be their primary task forever. Parents are also thinking about changes in their own lives, both personal and career-wise, and they may be readjusting their expectations regarding life. Change and instability are present in both generations!

It is this developmental perspective, however, that forms the tasks of the family at any particular stage of the life cycle, and eventually defines the role of the counselor in family therapy. L'abate, Ganahl, and Hansen describe the tasks for the family with adolescents in their book *Methods of Family Therapy.* "The family has to modify the parent-child relationship to permit the adolescent to move in and out of the family system. The boundaries must be more permeable because the parents can no longer maintain complete authority." Of course, this is more easily said than done, and a significant number of families can use the help of a counselor in order to accomplish this goal.

In practical terms, the work done by a lay counselor using the developmental perspective to family counseling may not *look* any different than the problem-solving approach. Using the example of the teenager in conflict with her parents over curfew, the developmental approach would suggest that the counselor help this family renegotiate curfew in light of this young girl's increasing acceptance of responsibility. This is similar to the activity of the problem-solving counselor.

Theoretically, however, there is a difference. The problem-solving counselor views the problem of curfew as obstructing the development of independence and responsibility. The developmentally oriented counselor sees such a problem as the consequence of developmental forces. Says Schultz, "Families in which the parents have over the years been able to influence and control the lives of their children appropriately are forced by the adolescent's push for independence to renegotiate power issues with the family, to endure the young person's healthy testing of limits, and, when necessary, to insist upon their adult prerogatives to still set the rules."

As youth workers counsel teenagers and their families, their role and goal of counseling when using the developmental perspective is as follows: *The lay counselor helps the family see the need for change and engages the family in counseling for the purpose of assisting family members to make the necessary changes in their parent-child relationships that allow for continued growth and development of the teenager.*

For the most part, lay counselors who choose to work with various members of a teenager's family will be working with relatively normal families who are experiencing common transitional problems. These problems are likely to arise as a teenager separates from parents and gravitates toward peers; disagrees with his parent's pacing of increased privileges and responsibilities; demands the right to make decisions regarding use of time, expenditure of money, and selection of friends; gives priority to individual needs over the needs of the family; questions the values of the family; and experiments with behavior that is not acceptable to parents.

Obviously, there will be many opportunities for counselors to work with families, either in helping them to solve specific problems, or to make changes that have been necessitated by the developmental forces leading to growth and development of the adolescent.

Who Is the Family?

It has become clear that the large, **extended family** of rural America is obsolete. It worked well when many hands were needed on the family farm or in the small family business. The pace of society was slow, and schedules were flexible and relatively free. Neighbors and relatives could drop by for a spontaneous visit, and members of a large family could gather together when the chores were done.

The **nuclear family,** parents and their children, has become the organizational pattern of urban society. With busy schedules, a fast pace, and little uncommitted time, it has become easier to manage with fewer people. This change means that a lesser number of people, however, must accomplish all the tasks required of the family regarding the growth and development of children.

Recognizing the members of a nuclear family is becoming more and more difficult in our changing society. Just a few decades ago, the family was composed of a husband and wife who had been married only to each other, and of their biological children. Organizationally, the mother and father of these children had distinct but complementary roles. The father worked outside of the home as the primary "provider," and the mother worked inside the home as the principal "nurturer" of the children's growth. This family pattern, however, is a thing of the past for the majority of American families. There are many alternative family patterns due to the breakup of many marriages and the need for both parents to work outside the home to make ends meet.

Despite all these changes and patterns, perhaps the essence of the family remains the same. Boyer and Jeffrey have described the family as well as anyone. "The family is a group of people living intimately together as a unit, sharing life's anticipations, disappointments, struggles, and joys. Complex communication skills connect unique individuals as the family grows and develops cohesiveness."

At the same time that the nature of the family is the same, it appears more difficult for families to accomplish their goals. As mentioned previously, the world in which the family lives is more complex, the component parts of the family are varied and often temporary, and there are fewer family members to finish the tasks.

In families with adolescents, the needs of the teenager often clash with the needs of the family. Teenagers need change, and families need stability. Dodson wrote in *Family Therapy: A Systems Approach,* "These dual, sometimes contrasting, human needs create the paradoxes of the family unit, in which exist struggle for separateness and togetherness, differentness and sameness, protection and freedom, support and independence."

As youth workers counseling families, it is important to recognize these conflicting needs, but it is just as important to recognize that society's patterns are often in conflict with the needs of a family. Just as a teenager is a part of the whole, families are an integral part of society. Although a family system may be changed through the work of a counselor in order to accommodate the growth needs of an adolescent, the counselor rarely is able to change society to accommodate the needs of the family.

The youth worker is primarily interested in the growth and development of teenagers with whom he or she works. Sometimes, however, counseling is done with parents apart from teens for the purpose of helping the family unit adapt and adjust to societal changes. And, in the long run, these changes will enable the family to continue to effectively provide for the needs of teenagers.

An example should help emphasize this point. In my counseling practice, I regularly see adults who maintain the traditional roles of parents, but who both work outside the home for economic reasons. It's the only way they can make ends meet in present-day America. What this means is that the wife continues to do the work inside the home and is the primary nurturer of the children. But, she must do all of this work after she has spent eight hours on the job outside the home. Her husband continues to be the primary provider, but he is through working when he gets home.

It becomes obvious that something has to give. This woman can not do it all. Nor should she. What usually gives is having enough time to monitor the children's activities and providing them with emotional support when they need it. This can become a critical problem for the family with teenagers. Remember, adolescents are in a tremendous period of change. They are trying new things, making decisions they haven't made before, all within the context of increased freedom and independence. What enables them to make these changes is the stability of the family.

Frank Pittman, in his book *Turning Points,* says, "There is no time in the life of a family when greater stability is required than during the adolescence of one of its members. Yet the adolescent offers no stability at all. The adolescent must derive stability from his or her family — it cannot come from within nor from equally unstable adolescent peers. However, if the parents are seen as thwarting change and growth toward independence, rather than tracking it, the parents cannot provide stability. Nor can the parents provide much stability while they are making their own marriage and life chaotic."

In our example, this family is having difficulty monitoring their children, not because they are directly thwarting change and growth toward independence, but because of changing societal economic patterns. A possible suggestion might be that the wife quit her job outside the home. Certainly this would enable at least one parent to monitor the adolescent and provide the stability necessary for continued growth and development. But, in today's circumstances, such a decision might mean the loss of the family home.

A counselor, aware of societal trends, may need to help these parents reconsider their traditional roles. Since both of them work outside the home in order to own their home, they might want to share the responsibilities at home, including the nurturance of their children. A counselor will find this a challenging task, but trying to change the economics of an entire nation is impossible! If and when this couple is able to make this key adjustment in their life-style, they will be better able to meet their own needs as well as those of their children.

In summary, families with teenagers are in transition. The youth worker who counsels adolescents will want to be aware of any family patterns that need adjusting due to societal changes that hinder the maintenance of stability. Helping parents make these adjustments will assist teenagers in their efforts to become mature adults.

Techniques of Family Counseling

Working with a teenager's family is a well-accepted concept when the problems and conflicts presented appear to be family-related. The lay counselor can use one of two approaches to family counseling: a problem-solving approach or a developmental approach. Additionally, when working with families, societal changes and pressures should be important considerations.

Once a family is engaged in counseling, there is the matter of what the counselor does to facilitate problem-solving or transitional changes. It is assumed that the counseling techniques described in chapter seven will be appropriately used in a family context. There are, however, some additional techniques that have been found to be effective tools when used with families.

Giving a Prescription

L'abate, Ganahl, and Hansen have defined a **prescription** as follows: "A prescription is a set of instructions or injunctions that the family is to follow at the request of the therapist." It may surprise the reader to learn that some counselors use prescriptions in light of the fact that counseling does not generally embrace the idea of telling a client what to do.

There are several reasons given, however, for justifying the use of a prescription when working with a family. First of all, the problem-solving approach to family counseling has been described as one in which the counselor actively intervenes in the life of a family. However, this is only done after the family has invited the counselor to help. They in effect have already given the counselor "permission" to actively get involved with them in finding solutions to their problems.

Second, a particular insight may have been discovered in a counseling session using the traditional techniques of counseling. What is said in a counseling session, however, is not always remembered or retained unless application is made at some later date or place. A prescription is a technique for getting family members to apply what they have learned in your office when they leave.

Third, a prescription at best is a request. There really isn't any way that a counselor can force a family to do what is asked unless they are willing to do so. In fact, the counselor can learn a lot about a family by watching to see if they follow through on a directive. Some think that a counselor will never really know if a family is willing to change unless a prescription is given.

Suppose that a family is trying to learn how to resolve a difference, and it becomes apparent in counseling that no one listens to what is being said. A prescription might sound like this: "During this next week, I want you to talk about how chores are assigned in your family. Make an effort to listen to each speaker before you give your opinion."

Perhaps you have been working with a family for the purpose of teaching its members to be more supportive of each other. Following a counseling session, you prescribe the following: "I want each of you to give every other member of the family a compliment this week."

The use of prescriptions can be a very effective technique for bringing about change in a family. Their use, however, should not take the place of families deciding on their own how they might change their relationships. Active involvement in finding solutions is what a counselor desires for a family, but the careful use of prescriptions can be very useful.

Assigning Homework

Homework assignments are typically tasks, exercises, and practice activities that are given to a family for the purpose of reinforcing something that has been learned in a counseling session. In the context of family counseling, they are usually tasks that enable family members to learn different and more productive ways of relating to each other.

Essentially, the rationale for using homework assignments is the same as that used for prescriptions. Many counselors use the two terms interchangeably. Those who make a distinction suggest that homework assignments are typically much more specific and/or elaborate. Whereas a prescription can be viewed to be similar to a doctor's brief instructions, an assignment can be seen as similar to an exercise assigned by a schoolteacher.

Homework assignments also suggest that what is learned will be done permanently. Suppose you are working with a teenager who rarely shares her opinion with other family members when plans are being made that involve everyone. When the time comes to implement the activity, she tells everyone that she doesn't want to go. The plans fall through as a result, and everyone is upset with her.

As the family's counselor, you want this young lady to learn the skill of asserting her opinion whenever the plans being made include and involve her. You want her to demonstrate this skill for the rest of her life, even when she has grown up and left home. Your homework assignment for this family is this: "When you make plans that involve every member of the family, I want each of you to turn to Marie and specifically ask her for her opinion. Marie, I am asking the family not to proceed until you have given your thoughts and feelings on the matter. I want you to particularly follow this assignment each time you are planning a family outing or a vacation."

Just like prescriptions, homework assignments can be very helpful as families learn new and constructive patterns of relating to each other. Families generally like homework assignments because it gives them something specific and concrete to do as a result of their work in a counseling session. These assignments also remind families that they are the key in bringing about important changes in the way they relate to each other. They can celebrate any success they achieve.

Role Playing

The technique of **role playing** is no doubt very familiar to most youth leaders. It's an activity that is often used in youth activities to get everyone involved in a more-or-less playful environment. It also breaks down defenses and resistance to change. Many of the same benefits occur when this technique is used in family counseling.

Perhaps the most notable feature of role playing is that it provides family members with an **experiential** way to understand their relationship patterns. Everyone can have a turn at experiencing what it must be like to be someone else in the family. Adolescents, in particular, can benefit from role playing because of their **egocentrism** in which they see everything through their own grid and don't pay much attention to the view of others. Role playing allows them to "get out of themselves" for a change.

Because role playing is experiential, it generally gets family members out of their heads and into their emotions. Although it isn't recommended by most mental health professionals for children in the primary grades, it can be an effective tool to involve families in the areas of their conflict, misunderstanding, and dysfunction.

The timeliness of role playing is important. In order for it to be effective, family members need to be willing to participate. To force someone to play a role can be destructive to the positive atmosphere of a family working together to effect change and growth. When members are willing, however, much can be accomplished in a relatively short amount of time.

L'abate, Ganahl, and Hansen suggest five types of roles that can help families experience new interactions for them:

1. *old roles versus new* — family members discard their old roles and assume completely new ones;
2. *actual roles versus fictional roles* — family members or the counselor create the make-believe ones;
3. *assumed roles versus assigned roles* — family members automatically assume some roles (i.e., peacemaker, rescuer) and are assigned others;
4. *same roles versus opposite roles* — family members play the roles they usually play and then are asked to play the opposite roles (i.e., child then parent);
5. *focused roles versus general roles* — family members first play roles that are general and somewhat irrelevant and then move to roles that are more specifically related to actual family roles.

Role playing is effective and easy to implement. Research confirms the fact that counselees believe that when a situation arises in their world that they have already rehearsed through role playing, the results are more positive. If a teenager is willing to participate, role playing is an excellent way to get him involved in a counseling session.

Sculpting the Family

The technique of **sculpting** is somewhat similar to role playing. It is an active, vital, experiential process that involves each member of the family in a unique way. The difference, however, is significant. Whereas family members play various roles in role playing, sculpting is a technique whereby one member of the family, the sculptor, arranges family members in a way that is expressive of the dynamics or relationship patterns of the family. For example, if a teenager feels as though he is alienated from the rest of the family, he may arrange the members of his family on one side of the room and move himself to the opposite side of the room. Or, if a teenage girl feels like she is often caught in the middle of her parents' arguments, she may arrange the family so that she is standing between her mother and father.

Teenagers often enjoy the process of sculpting, and they can be more willing and expressive than adults. Actually, various family members are usually asked to sculpt the family, as each member experiences family relationships a bit differently than the others. It is probably best to ask for a volunteer sculptor.

The counselor's role during sculpting is to monitor the process, keep its focus sharp, ask for clarification if the arrangement is unclear, and change the picture to a new problem or relationship pattern when appropriate. And, of course, the counselor will eventually help the family members explore and discuss what they experienced and felt. It is even helpful at times to have a sculptor arrange the family in a new pattern that he or she would like to see.

Sculpting is a dynamic, novel, active technique to help families see their negative and destructive relationship patterns. It actually allows them to "see" what their family looks like in terms of its functioning. It can be eye-opening, and it can also serve to motivate needed change. As in role playing, it is an excellent device to get teenagers involved.

Writing a Contract

Finally, the technique of having family members design and sign a **contract** has been found to be particularly useful with teenagers. A contract is basically an agreement. Since parents and adolescents often must negotiate rules, privileges, and responsibilities, contractual methods are useful and effective methods for bringing about needed changes in the parent-child relationship.

Counselors can help adolescents and their parents write contracts in which teenagers may participate in extracurricular activities as long as they complete assigned work at home. Maybe a teenager obtains the use of a car as long as his school grades are a B average or better. Or, a teenager can have her own phone as long as she limits its use to a few specified hours during the day. The possibilities are limitless.

Writing and agreeing to contracts is generally a positive experience for teenagers and their parents. Although everyone has to give something, everyone also gets something. Everyone comes out a winner. Additionally, putting contracts in writing decreases the possibility of misunderstanding in the future. The use of contracts can be a very effective way to get families to change their relationship patterns.

Resistant Family Members

Some professional counselors refuse to see family members unless all members participate in family counseling. Others do not take such a rigid position on the matter. It would be difficult for a lay counselor to take the stance that all family members must be involved. These counselors typically play a variety of roles with teenagers and their parents, and a rigid stance on the matter might alienate the youth worker from the family. It is better to attempt to get as many family members involved as is appropriate or possible rather than delay or refuse counseling entirely.

The ideal, however, is to have all family members from the very beginning of the counseling process, and make every effort to keep everyone involved until counseling is completed. Some counselors who fail to get all family members present suggest using an "empty chair." The chair represents the absent family member, and the counselor can always ask others present what the missing family member would think, feel, or do. Dodson suggests asking family members to play the role of an absent member. Or the counselor can simply ask those present questions about the missing family member.

The general guideline is to get all members to participate when it is believed that a teenager's problems are family related. Make a phone call, write a note, or get the other family members to accept the responsibility to bring an individual. If all else fails, however, work with as many of the adolescent's family as possible.

Family counseling is an effective strategy whenever a teenager's problems, difficulties, and conflicts are enmeshed with interaction patterns of the family. In these circumstances, counseling the teenager alone is rarely successful in the long run. He is not strong enough to change family interaction patterns by himself. The counselor who can involve the entire family when it is appropriate can be an effective change agent on behalf of the teenager and his family.

Ten

CRISIS
INTERVENTION
COUNSELING

Youth workers performing the role of a lay counselor are very likely to come in contact with teenagers in crisis. This is the natural consequence of working with adolescents where they live. The mere use of the word *crisis* can be enough to raise the anxiety level of counselors and cause them to question their ability to help teenagers when teenagers are unable to help themselves. Fortunately, crises are temporary, and teenagers can be helped over these hurdles with care and competency.

Understanding the nature of a crisis and learning how to intervene effectively can reduce anxiety and increase self-confidence. It is reassuring, for example, to know that there are identifiable phases of **crisis intervention** counseling, and there are particular things to do during each phase that help to bring about resolution of a crisis. Also, there are several counseling strategies that help to hasten the return of a teenager to a normal state of functioning. It can be very satisfying to realize that in addition to teenagers being helped through a crisis period, they are likely to learn new coping skills that serve to prevent a similar crisis in the future.

What Is a Crisis?

Mental health professionals have defined a crisis as a period of time in which an individual cannot handle a situation or circumstance by means of his or her current resources or coping strategies. Caplan, in *An Approach to Community Mental Health,* describes a crisis as a time "when a person faces an obstacle to important life goals that is, for a time, insurmountable through the utilization of his customary methods of problem solving." Notice that a crisis is not necessarily perceived by counseling professionals as an illness or a pathological response.

A helpful way for lay counselors to view a crisis is to think of it as a temporary period of time when the skill level of the teenager is inadequate for the size of the problem being faced. The nature of crisis intervention counseling, therefore, is to assist the teenager through this period and to help the teenager increase his or her skill level in order to handle similarly sized problems in the future.

Types of Crises

Some crises are developmental in nature in that they occur during transitional periods of an individual's life. Interestingly, Pittman has labeled an entire section "Crises of Development" in his book *Turning Points: Treating Families in Transition and Crisis.* He suggests that there are four transition periods when crises may appear: (1) when an adult becomes a parent, (2) when a child becomes an adolescent, (3) when the children of parents leave home, and (4) when an adult becomes elderly.

Adolescents can experience developmental crises initiated by having to take gang showers for the first time on entrance to junior high school, needing to make all new friends in an unfamiliar senior high school, or having to adjust to living with one parent following a divorce. These transitional experiences can be anticipated or unexpected. In any case, each requires the teenager to respond to circumstances for which he or she may be inadequately skilled or prepared to handle.

Other crises are situational in nature. They are events that occur in the life of a teenager. Crises of this type can be initiated when a teenager's father becomes unemployed and the family is homeless, when a teenager's identity is tied to athletics and a sports injury occurs, when a teenage girl is raped, when a healthy adolescent contracts a serious, life-threatening illness, when there is a premature death of a parent or sibling, when a comfortable, long-term relationship with a member of the opposite sex is unexpectedly ended, or when a teenager fails to make the team or be selected as a cheerleader, or win an election. Some situational crises result from natural disasters such as earthquakes, floods, or hurricanes.

Stages of a Crisis

It appears as though individuals who experience a crisis go through a series of steps. Golan identified five component parts in his book *Treatment in Crisis Situations*. The first stage is the **hazardous event.** Regardless of its nature, developmental or situational, the event is extremely threatening and stressful to the individual. It interrupts the natural flow of life and is experienced as overwhelming by the person. The second stage is the **vulnerable state,** which refers to the individual's reaction to the stressful event. The person begins to figure out what to do in response to the hazardous event. If during this stage the person is able to find an adequate way to cope with the stressful event, movement to an active crisis is unlikely. If normal means for coping are inadequate, however, the individual is very vulnerable to crisis development.

The third component leading to a crisis is the **precipitating factor.** Although it is possible for a stressful event to be so powerful that it causes a state of disequilibrium by itself, such an unfolding of events is not common. Certainly natural disasters can be so devastating that a crisis occurs immediately. In the life of a teenager, however, most situational and developmental situations are less powerful. Usually, there are several events, and the one that finally brings on an active crisis state is known as the precipitating factor.

I remember an adolescent boy who was involved in a car accident as a sophomore in high school. He experienced facial damage, which necessitated plastic surgery. His doctor explained to the family that this type of surgery must be done through a series of scheduled surgeries. This young man's accident was the hazardous event. In order, his first operation occurred on the night of his accident; he had to stay in the hospital for a time of recuperation; he had to make several adjustments in his diet and method of eating due to a wired-shut jaw; he had to face his friends on his return to school; and he faced his second surgery. Although difficult and challenging, he managed to get through these phases of his recovery fairly well. And then came his third surgery. Evidently, he had used up all his energy reserve and coping strategies. It was as though he had reached the last straw, and he had nothing left to maintain a sense of equilibrium. His third surgery became the precipitating factor. A temporary crisis was the result.

Golan called the fourth stage an **active crisis state.** This is the period in which the individual experiences the most pain and greatest sense of disequilibrium. It feels as though life is out of control, and there is no apparent way to solve the situation. There can be physiological symptoms such as shortness of breath, rapid heartbeat, increased blood pressure, and increased perspiration. Emotionally, the person can feel a sense of panic, impending doom, anxiety, depression, anger, inadequacy, hopelessness, and/or confusion. It may be difficult for the person to think and process what steps might be taken to alleviate the crisis. No one person need experience all of these symptoms, but most people in crisis experience a combination of several of them.

Finally, the individual enters the **reintegration** stage. There is a reduction of stress, and the person can begin to see the end of the crisis. A sense of equilibrium returns, and it is possible for the person to begin to evaluate the crisis and develop new coping skills for future use. A return to a normal level of functioning occurs. The crisis ends.

The Steps of Crisis Intervention
The steps of crisis intervention serve to reach two major goals: (1) to alleviate the stress symptoms and restore a sense of equilibrium to the teenager, and (2) to help the adolescent assess the crisis and develop coping mechanisms that can be used to prevent a recurrence in the future. This process is short-term intervention that purposes to help the teenager over a temporary hurdle so that normal development can continue.

Solid crisis intervention counseling usually takes from four to six face-to-face contacts before an individual adequately works through a crisis. The first contact should occur as quickly as possible on learning of a crisis in order to provide help to a teenager during a time of instability. It is wise to schedule contacts fairly close together in order to minimize rapid deterioration of the situation. The counselor will want to be more available to the teenager in crisis than is usually the case, and phone contacts for added support between face-to-face contacts can prove reassuring.

Each contact with a teenager in crisis will need to be used efficiently and effectively. The point is to get the teenager stabilized and back on a normal course with dispatch. During the first contact, the counselor will want to center attention on the nature of the crisis, the state of the counselee, and an agreement to work together toward resolution of the crisis. The next several contacts will focus on the steps necessary to resolve the crisis and to implement the intervention plan. The last contact or two will be spent assessing the crisis and noting coping strategies that can be used in the future. Golan describes these three phases of crisis intervention as **formulation, implementation,** and **termination.**

Naturally, the intervention plan will be appropriate to the nature of the crisis, and it will be based on the strengths and limitations of the counselee, the physical and emotional states of the teenager, the supporting elements surrounding the individual (parents, teachers, friends), and the resources in the community (doctors, mental health professionals, the courts, other community agencies). In contrast to other types of counseling, the counselor will be quite active and directive in the development and implementation of any intervention plan. The teenager in crisis is beyond his or her ability to cope and the counselor therefore takes more responsibility.

Counseling Techniques

As it is true in other counseling situations, there are several counseling techniques that have proven to be effective strategies for crisis intervention work. Obviously, a teenager in crisis is going to benefit greatly from a counselor who listens empathetically to what is happening and who is supportive and encouraging. This is not the time to probe, reflect, confront, evaluate, or interpret, particularly during the first several contacts with the person in crisis. Individuals in crisis are unsure of the outcome facing them and their ability to survive.

These individuals may feel anxious, depressed, hopeless. Their safety, health, and welfare may be in danger. They feel as though they are in a problem that is insurmountable. They are not at all sure they are going to make it. They may become suicidal in order to escape the intense pressure and stress they are experiencing. These people can be greatly reassured to know that a counselor believes they can overcome their present difficulties. A counselor's calm, methodical, directive approach can help them regain perspective on the crisis at hand.

Crisis intervention counseling is one of the few times when a counselor can get away with a direct approach. During the active crisis state, an individual is much more open to the direct assistance of another person. Hollis, writing in *Casework: A Psychosocial Therapy*, suggested that direct influence is an important and effective strategy for working with people in crisis. These are times when it can often be appropriate to give advice, to indicate what a counselee should do, to direct the behavior of the individual. Such individuals are often confused and have difficulty knowing what they need to do in order to successfully face their crisis. The counselor therefore makes suggestions that are in the best interest of the person.

Crises are also times when a counselor may take steps to directly intervene in the life of a teenager. These steps are taken particularly when a teenager's safety, health, and welfare are in danger (i.e., rape, sexual molestation, homelessness, suicide). Direct intervention often takes the form of a team approach. For example, a crisis may dictate

111

working with a young girl's family on learning that she is pregnant. Reporting to a child protective agency (police, courts, welfare, or probation departments) may be necessitated on learning that a teenage girl has been raped. Contacting a community agency may help get a homeless family off the street. Taking an adolescent to the emergency room of a local hospital is warranted in view of a drug overdose. Referring a family to a mental health professional is strongly recommended when a teenager appears severely depressed and suicidal. Collaborating with school personnel may help the teenager who has recently moved to town and is having trouble coping with her new school surroundings. These are all examples of when it is appropriate to use the vast resources of a community that surround a teenager.

As the teenager begins to stabilize and regain a sense of equilibrium, the more traditional counseling techniques discussed earlier can be used to help the adolescent assess the crisis just passed and develop new coping strategies. These counseling techniques can help the teenager see the crisis from a new perspective, determine various alternatives and courses of action that can be implemented independently, understand the physical and emotional responses to the crisis, and develop new skills for use in the future. For example, a teenager who experienced a crisis on entering high school may want to learn a variety of new behaviors that are helpful in making and maintaining new friendships.

All the counseling strategies used in crisis intervention work are implemented in the context of short-term intervention. Long term, insight counseling done for the purpose of making major changes in one's attitudes, relationship patterns, and behavior is not the purpose. There will be other opportunities for this type of counseling. For the moment, the point is to help a teenager back on track and beyond the crisis situation.

A Sample Case of Crisis Intervention

One of the adolescent girls in your youth group was recently diagnosed as having a brain tumor. In a matter of a few short weeks, this teenager had surgery for the removal of the tumor, recuperated in the hospital, and was released into the care of her parents at home. Although she wanted to return to school immediately in order to see her friends, she was ordered by her doctor to continue her recuperation at home until her strength returned.

Finally the day arrived when this emerging adult was given her doctor's approval to return to school. As her youth worker, you hear about this good news from one of her friends who also attends your youth group. You call her to congratulate her and tell her that you will be thinking about her during her first day back at school. She sounds excited at the prospect of seeing her friends again. Her day at school went well although she was very tired by the end of the day. Her teachers and friends were delighted to see her, and she was glad to be back. Upon calling her on the phone the same evening, she tells you that her day had been "great."

HAZARDOUS EVENT: A LIFE-THREATENING ILLNESS

A few days later, you receive an urgent call from this young lady's mother. You learn that her daughter refuses to go to school, doesn't respond to reminders that she is already behind in her subjects, stays in her room most of the day, is alternately depressed and angry, says that "nothing matters anymore," and is writing poetry with suicidal overtones. Her mother sounds frightened and tells you that her husband and she don't know what to do. She urgently pleads that you talk with their daughter by telling you that her daughter says that you are the only person with whom she will talk. You agree to see this young girl the same day as the phone call from her mother.

First Contact. In a supportive, reassuring manner, you ask this young lady in your office to describe what happened. You learn from her that she was in school one day and had just entered her afternoon humanities class. A couple of her friends were talking about a career unit they had just completed, and they wanted to know what she saw herself doing in the future. She explains, "Suddenly, I realized I might not have a future. I got real scared, and my mind went blank. I started to cry and couldn't stop. I couldn't help it. I couldn't breathe. I had to get out of there. I ran out of the classroom, called my mother, and she came and took me home."

PRECIPITATING FACTOR: QUESTION ABOUT THE FUTURE

Although you will have had to help elicit the responses of this young girl, you already know the precipitating factor and her emotional response to it. Now you need to know something of the background that led up to her active crisis state. Perhaps you ask her, "Can you remember when you started worrying about the future?"

In listening to this frightened teenager, you learn the context of her present crisis. "At first, I was just glad to get home from the hospital. So much had happened to me so fast. Learning I had a tumor on my brain. Waking up in the hospital room after surgery. Frustrated that I couldn't go home. Finally, my parents took me home. I wanted to go to school right away, but my doctor wouldn't let me until I got stronger." You urge her to continue by saying, "That sounds like a really frightening experience. Then what happened?"

"At first I couldn't have visitors. That really made me mad. My parents kept telling me I needed my rest. Didn't they know that I needed my friends? They treated me like I was an invalid. They wouldn't let me do anything. But, when I would try to do something, I would get tired really fast. It was really frustrating! My father told me that if I didn't take it easy, I might get sick again. At first, I thought that was stupid, but I began wondering about it. I didn't tell anyone. Do you think my tumor will grow back? My doctor tells me everything is OK, but I would just die if he told me it had. Even when I went back to school, my parents would look worried every time I caught them looking at me."

"How did you feel during this time?" you ask her. "It got really scary. I tried not to think about it. It was like I was in a daze. When my doctor said I could go back to school, though, I forgot about it for a few days. Until I went to my class and my friends asked me what I wanted to do with my future. That's when I lost it."

VULNERABLE STATE: SHOCK ("I WAS IN A DAZE.")

Now you want to look at how she is doing at present. You ask her, "What's it like now?" You learn the following from her: "I just can't make myself do anything. I'm not going back to school. I'm so embarrassed. Who cares, anyway? I'll probably be dead soon anyway. My folks tell me I need to do my schoolwork. Why should I? I'm so angry! A few weeks ago life seemed great. And then I have a brain tumor. Most of the time, though, I feel depressed. It's like this thing comes down over me. I just sit and stare. My folks seem really worried. You can see it in their eyes. Sometimes I think that it would be better if I could just close my eyes and it would be over. I'm just so confused! I just want everything to be like it was. I don't know what to do."

At this point, you will probably want to assess the possibility of suicide. Contrary to popular belief, asking an individual if he is thinking about killing himself will not encourage him to try it. Instead, it brings the thought out in the open, often diffuses its power, and reduces the pain of the individual. This teenager says in answer to your question, "It crosses my mind once in a while, mostly in my poetry. What I really want to do is go back to school with my friends, but it is just so hard. I'm so scared."

ACTIVE CRISIS STATE: DEPRESSED, CONFUSED, ANGRY, SUICIDAL IDEAS

As this first contact comes to a close, you make every attempt to reassure this young girl that things will improve. Let her know that you are ready to help her, and that you want to see her in a day or two so that you can plan with her the steps that will get her back to school and on her way again. Be positive, but realistic. Get her to commit to working with you by scheduling your next meeting. Let her know that you will call her tonight just so that you can keep in touch. Give her your phone number and give her permission to call if she needs to do so.

Second through Fourth Contacts. Prior to this second meeting, you have called a mental health professional you know to discuss this young teenager's depression and **suicidal ideation.** You want to know if it is recommended that this young lady see a professional counselor. You are told that her level of depression, refusal to go to school, emotional instability, and suicidal ideation merits recommending to the family that she visit a counseling professional.

During these sessions, you will be learning about this girl's strengths and weaknesses, her energy level, the coping mechanisms that have been successful in the past, and her support system. You learn the following about her:

1. She is not an initiator but responds well to others' initiation.
2. She seems to spend an inordinate amount of time thinking about the future, but doesn't always enjoy the present as much as she could.
3. She works best with others but loses motivation when having to work alone.
4. She works best when given clear directions about short-term tasks. She loses focus when working on long-term projects without much direction.
5. She responds well to praise but has difficulty with criticism.

Let this teenager know that you believe she has some personality characteristics that you know will help her through this difficult time and get her back on track. Together you decide to work toward the following immediate goals:

1. Begin work with a counseling professional to reduce her symptoms of depression. (Be sure to get the cooperation of her parents.)
2. Re-establish her contacts with her peers in order for her to regain their emotional support.
3. Return to school and become a productive student as she was in the past.
4. Begin to understand her emotional responses to the question regarding her future.

Notice that each of these goals is clear, realistic, and immediately attainable within the time frame of four to six contacts. She will begin work with a counselor, re-establish peer contacts, return to school, and understand her emotional responses. In order to accomplish these goals, there will be steps for you, as her lay counselor, to complete, as well as tasks for her and her parents to finish.

The following tasks are assigned for completion during the second through fourth contacts.

The Lay Counselor:

1. Refer this teenager's family to a professional counselor you know and trust.
2. Discuss with her parents the need to begin treating her as normally as possible, such as requiring her to follow through on her regular chores and responsibilities.
3. Call her counselor at school. Share what you have found out about her strengths and weaknesses. Suggest that teachers give her assignments, at least until the crisis is over, that are clear, task-oriented, and done in a small group context. Provide a lot of praise and minimize criticism.
4. Ask two of her best friends to pick her up and bring her to your youth group meetings.
5. Suggest to her parents that they inform their daughter's medical doctor of this crisis intervention plan, including the fact that his patient will be seeing a mental health professional.

The Teenager:

1. She will call her two or three closest friends and tell them that she is now able to talk on the phone at night during a specified period of time.
2. She will make every effort to attend the youth group meetings with her friends.
3. She will make arrangements, with the help of her parents, to drive to and from school with several of her school friends.
4. She will make every effort to attend her scheduled counseling sessions with her professional counselor.
5. She will promise to report to you her progress to date during your meetings with her.

Her Parents:

1. They will make arrangements for counseling with a professional counselor and participate in that process as recommended by their counselor.
2. They will begin to return to an atmosphere of normalcy at home, treating their daughter in a way that gives her reassurance and confidence.
3. They will discuss their fears and uncertainty with their daughter's medical doctor, the professional counselor, or you.
4. They will praise their daughter for her efforts to re-establish her peer relationships and return to school.

Fifth and Sixth Contacts. During these contacts, you and this young lady will monitor the progress being made. Any adjustments that need to be made will be considered and implemented. As she returns to a sense of equilibrium, begin to discuss the crisis in retrospect, observing the degree to which she views the series of events leading to the crisis in a more realistic way. Help her to see various alternatives for dealing with a similar but different event in the future. For example, she may be able to see that her overemphasis on the future may be misguided. No one has a guarantee regarding the future. As an immature teenager with all of life ahead of her, she thought life would go on forever. Learning to be more "now-oriented," the only time that is certain, may help her deal more effectively with an uncertain future. She may also want to explore the fact that she depends on others for her emotional support, and she places the responsibility on them to meet her needs. (She is a responder, not an initiator.) When combined with the fact that her illness separated her from those on whom she depended, she had no internal source of emotional support to carry her through a very difficult time in her life. Learning to accept more responsibility for herself may be an important coping mechanism for her to develop.

REINTEGRATION: RETURN TO STABILITY AND ATTAINMENT OF NEW COPING STRATEGIES

When the goals of crisis intervention work have been met, it is time to terminate the intervention plan. Continuing to work with this teenager following the successful completion of the goals is unnecessary and can lead to a dependency relationship. The goal is for her to once again function in a relatively independent manner consistent with her abilities and maturity level. When the crisis is over, crisis intervention counseling stops.

A youth worker can provide invaluable assistance to a teenager in crisis. Individuals are open to help in the midst of a crisis. You are already a trusted adult in the lives of teenagers, and they are likely to want and need your help when they hit an obstacle that appears insurmountable to them. You can help them through this period and help them on their way.

Eleven

ADOLESCENT DISTURBANCES NEEDING SPECIAL CARE

Youth workers and lay counselors for the most part will work with adolescents who are experiencing the typical difficulties of growing up in a complex world. It isn't easy to attain the knowledge and skill adults need for successful and fulfilled living. Questions about self, others, and the world abound in the minds of teenagers, and it takes a good while to integrate the answers. Adults who work with youth are in a great position to come alongside these vulnerable but relatively healthy young people whenever there are blocks and hurdles standing in the way of growth and development.

There are times, however, when a youth worker will face a teenager who is in serious trouble. These adolescents are no longer experiencing a simple challenge to growth but are exhibiting strong behavioral disturbances or are faced with circumstances that are beyond the norm of healthy development. The lay counselor will benefit by having a general background regarding these problems and a set of guidelines for working with these young people.

118

Four problem areas are becoming so prevalent among teenagers that the youth worker is likely to come face-to-face with any one of them sooner or later. These issues are teenage depression, suicide, pregnancy, and drug abuse. Although these circumstances are difficult and at times beyond the scope of a youth worker's level of expertise, troubled adolescents can greatly benefit from a lay counselor's care, concern, and skill. Working in concert with counseling professionals and an array of community agencies, a youth worker can help alleviate the pain and confusion experienced by these emerging adults. Entire books have been written describing these problems in great detail. You may want to refer to these resources for a more detailed understanding of these adolescent problems.

Depression

Most people have experienced a lowering of mood at one time or another. Circumstances, disappointments, or the loss of a loved one can lead to **depression.** These emotional lows, however, are usually transitory and abate over time as adjustments are made. To be clinically depressed, however, can severely impact one's view of life and ability to take care of oneself, cause social and occupational dysfunction, and lead to suicide if left untreated. Naturally, there are levels of severity, but severe clinical depression can have tragic consequences.

Clinical depression is known by mental health professionals as a Mood Disorder. Although it is characterized by a depressed mood, there is actually a constellation of symptoms that constitute a depressive syndrome. Not everyone who is depressed will have them all, but these symptoms include a depressed mood or loss of interest in life, decreased interest in one's usual activities, eating disturbances (compulsive eating or loss of appetite), sleep disturbances, a loss of energy, withdrawal from others, feelings of alienation, worthlessness, hopelessness, and guilt, an inability to concentrate or think, and suicidal thoughts or actions, all leading to social and occupational dysfunction.

It is difficult to diagnose adolescent depression for several reasons. First of all, adolescents are experiencing many feelings for the first time, a natural result of the developmental process. It is often difficult for them to recognize or even label accurately the emotions they are feeling. Second, normal adolescents experience mood swings, including depressed moods. They can be on top of the world one moment, and in the pits the next! A poor grade on an exam can be "the worst moment of my life," and a phone call from a best friend can bolster a flagging self-esteem. Third, the mere fact of development, which thrusts teenagers into temporary phases of life in which they are unfamiliar, can lead to feelings of inadequacy and inferiority.

119

Such feelings can serve as the catalyst for feelings of depression and hopelessness. Life can feel pretty overwhelming at times.

Clinical depression in teenagers, however, does present some clues when the adult is sensitive to them and a keen observer of adolescent behavior. Teenage depression is often expressed in irritability, antisocial behavior, alcohol and drug use (an attempt to self-medicate to deaden the pain), withdrawal from peers and significant adults, a breakdown of communication lines, feelings of alienation ("No one understands me or cares about me"), a drop in the usual level of academic performance, an inability to concentrate, a proneness to accidents, alternating feelings of anger and depression, apathy, restlessness, boredom, and inattention to physical appearance. Obviously, these symptoms make it difficult for teenagers to function effectively or relate normally to those around them.

For a period of time, adolescents may be able to cope with these feelings and symptoms. Over a longer period of time, however, their coping mechanisms deteriorate and they experience feelings of hopelessness and despair. They feel like failures, as though their inability to do simple tasks or remember details is the result of personal flaws in their personality. Their self-esteem drops, and they can become depressed or angry because of their inability to deal effectively with their circumstances. Most teenagers, if they could, would describe their situation simply: "It hurts."

Major depression is generally treated in one of two major ways, or by a combination of both. The first approach is medication, which must be prescribed by a medical doctor (psychiatrist). The second approach is a type of counseling known as **cognitive therapy.** Pioneered by Aaron Beck and others, this approach is based on the idea that one's cognitions (thoughts) determine how a person feels. Burns, in his book *Feeling Good,* described depressed people as having thought patterns that are incredibly negative and pessimistic, patterns which are extremely distorted and exaggerated. For example, a teenager who doesn't get a desired "A" grade on a paper actually experiences the grade as though it were a failure.

Mental health professionals who implement cognitive therapy propose to restructure the thought patterns of a person in such a way that they are balanced and more in line with reality. The result is a changed thought process, and the previous depression lifts in response to this change. Other feelings, more in line with the person's cognitions, are the result. As was previously mentioned, sometimes cognitive therapy and medication are combined.

Guidelines for Lay Counselors
Depressed adolescents want to feel better. Sometimes the severity of their depression, however, makes it difficult—if not impossible—for

them to improve without the assistance of a caring counselor. Youth workers can be of significant help to these hurting young people. The following guidelines are given for consideration.

1. Be a helpful and concerned listener. Depressed teenagers often feel as though no one cares about them. They tend to withdraw from those who might help them, and they internalize their pain. Taking the initiative to talk and listen to them can help them express their feelings. It can also help them realize that someone does care about what is happening to them. This alone can reduce their pain.

2. Ask them if they have considered suicide. The majority of suicidal individuals experience significant depression. If a teenager admits to suicidal thoughts or exhibits suicidal clues, follow the steps listed in the "Preventing Adolescent Suicide" section later in this chapter.

3. Accept teenagers' feelings without judgment. It is extremely important that adolescents feel acceptance. Any form of judgment will hinder any further discussion. Depressed teenagers' feelings are very real to them, and a counselor must not minimize or invalidate them.

4. Consult with and/or refer to a counseling professional. Describe clearly and as completely as possible the teenager's symptoms, including any suicidal thoughts or actions. Ask whether or not professional counseling is recommended. Follow through on any recommendations received. This may mean getting the teenager's parents involved.

5. Explore with mildly depressed teenagers the possible causes of the depression. Suggest alternate ways to view or respond to external circumstances, and look at possible actions the teenagers might take to change these circumstances.

6. Provide continued support to the teenagers whose depression is serious enough to warrant professional counseling. Ending contact following a referral to a counseling professional may seem to an adolescent that you no longer care. Ongoing support is crucial to recovery.

7. Keep the depressed teenagers involved with other members of your youth group. Activity can energize depressed people. Also, hurting teenagers can benefit from the energy of friends, and such participation can reduce the tendency to withdraw.

8. Try to get the teenager involved in physical activity or exercise. Increased oxygen increases the energy level of a person. This can help lift a teenager's depression.

9. Celebrate a depressed teenager's recovery! Be thankful that God allowed you to be a part of the healing process. Enjoy the teenager's return to healthy living.

Suicide

Suicide among teenagers has risen dramatically in the past few years. According to *Vital Statistics in the United States 1960–1980,* suicide has become the third most common cause of deaths among adolescents aged 15–19. The rate of suicide in this age group has risen 300 percent in the last 20 years. In fact, the greatest increase in suicide rates recently has been among 15–24-year-old adolescents.

These numbers, however, only reflect the known suicides. It is believed by many medical authorities that many accidents are actually suicide cases. There just isn't any hard evidence to confirm the suicide at the site of the accident. The truth is that more and more adolescents are ending their lives at the very time when we would expect them to be filled with promise.

In spite of these dreary statistics, there is hope for these young people as long as we can identify them and provide the help they need. Suicidal people are quite ambivalent about ending their lives. In fact, 80 percent of those people who committed suicide gave some type of warning to those around them. Polly Joan, a coordinator of a suicide prevention and crisis service and author of *Preventing Teenage Suicide,* says: "It is not that they want to die, they just can't think of any other way to stop the pain." This is where the caring youth worker can enter the picture. The lay counselor can assist these young people to see and consider other options.

Causes of Suicide

There is no single factor causing suicide. There are usually a combination of factors that lead to suicidal thinking and behavior. In his book *Attack on the Self,* Miller says that "changes in society have made adolescence into an excessively complicated developmental period." He lists several social determinants of suicide: (1) disintegration of the nuclear and extended family units which traditionally provided emotional support and a variety of adult role models, (2) deterioration of shared parenting due to separation and divorce, which makes it difficult to resolve sexual and personal issues, (3) attitudes of society, which have tended to minimize the value of human life and the need to accept responsibility for one another, (4) society's difficulty in handling death, which makes it harder for teenagers to resolve their own significant losses, and (5) the increased availability of the means to suicide, particularly drugs and guns.

Polly Joan would add to this list the fact that teenagers experience tremendous expectations to succeed, feel great pressure to make vast choices in a complicated world, often blame themselves for their family's conflicts and struggles, and face a world whose future is clouded and uncertain. Is it any wonder that the rate of teenage suicide is rising?

When contemplating possible causes of suicide, various emotional and psychological factors should be considered. For instance, studies show that between 50 and 80 percent of suicidal individuals experience significant depression. Adolescents are vulnerable to depression when they feel inadequate and face extremely difficult situations beyond their control. These young people can feel hopeless to the point of despair if they see no way out of their current circumstances. Sensitive adolescents caught up in so much pain can see themselves as failures, distancing themselves from those around them. They become lonely and alienated. Finally, they can begin to consider suicide as the only option for ending their pain.

Several factors appear to increase the likelihood of suicide: (1) teens who historically have had difficulty in school and their social relationships and have a low sense of self-esteem, (2) teens who have experienced a series of disappointments, including a significant loss, (3) teens who have previously attempted suicide or whose parent committed suicide, (4) teens who experience significant depression, and (5) teens suffering from a serious illness. Interestingly, the rate of suicide is higher for males than for females, and the rate is higher among whites than nonwhites.

Preventing Adolescent Suicide

There are several things a youth worker can do to help the adolescent contemplating suicide. First, listen to the teenager's pain. These young people carry their pain alone. Because they have distanced themselves from others, their normal system of communication with others has been disconnected. They have no one to talk to and believe that no one really cares. In the process of internalizing their pain, they are unable to **reality test** their perceptions about their world. They therefore distort and exaggerate their circumstances and see no alternative except suicide.

An empathetic, supportive listener can do much to ease the pain. In fact, talking about their pain sometimes is all that is needed to diffuse suicidal feelings. Teenagers do not want to die, but they are in need of relief. Their pain has some basis to it, and a full measure of support from a caring youth leader can be crucial to preventing suicide. As the counselor listens to a teenager's pain, statements such as these are helpful: "Man, that must really hurt." "I can see why you feel as you do." "That would hurt anybody." These statements will not justify suicide in the minds of teenagers. Instead, they let teens know that someone understands their situation.

Second, talk to the teenager about suicide if you suspect depression or notice hints of potential suicide. It is helpful to be direct. It is alright to ask, "Have you thought about killing yourself?" Talking to teenagers about self-destructive thoughts will not serve to put the idea in their minds, nor will it cause teenagers to commit suicide. On the contrary, bringing these thoughts into the open provides relief from the building pressure that results from keeping them inside.

Third, listen to the suicidal ideas presented by the teenager. Are the thoughts fleeting or constant? Has a suicide plan been devised? How elaborate is the plan? How lethal is the method? Has there been a history of suicide in the teenager's family? Has the teenager attempted suicide previously? Is the person rigid or flexible? To what degree does the teenager have control of impulses? How alienated is the adolescent from family and friends? The answers to these questions will help you know what to do, and assist you in consulting with a counseling professional regarding the teenager.

Fourth, take every step necessary to prevent a suicide. A youth worker can really help the teenager who is mildly depressed, may have a few fleeting suicidal thoughts, but has no intention or plan. Scheduling a few counseling sessions can help these young people explore the possible reasons for their depression and look at alternate methods of coping with their stress. Counselors would be wise to let these adolescents know that any promises regarding confidentiality are null and void if they intend to harm themselves. Such a statement can serve to let teenagers know how much you value their lives. Continue to monitor these teenagers in case their depression increases.

If a teenager is moderately or severely depressed, take all of the steps listed earlier in the "Depression" section. Talk, listen, consult with a mental health professional, notify parents, refer for counseling, and continue support. If you fear that a teenager's attempt to commit suicide is imminent, there is a variety of actions to consider immediately.

1. Call a crisis hotline for suggestions and recommendations.
2. Immediately contact the teenager's parents.
3. Keep talking to the teenager on the phone until the crisis is over. Immediately schedule a time to get together as soon as possible.
4. Do not leave the teenager alone. Arrange for a relative or a friend to stay with the teenager.
5. Call a few hours following the crisis to make sure the teenager is doing fine.
6. Attempt to remove or have the teenager destroy the means of suicide. For example, "I want you to flush the pills down the toilet. Go do it now, and then come back and tell me they are gone."
7. Get a verbal agreement that the teenager will not attempt suicide without first talking to you in person.

8. Make arrangements for the teenager to see a counseling professional immediately. Work in concert with the teenager's parents.
9. Take the teenager to the emergency room of the hospital.
10. Call the police and have them meet you at the teenager's house.

The point is simple. *Do whatever you need to do to avert the crisis.* Don't worry about making a mistake or overreacting. If you think the danger of suicide is imminent, don't worry about overreacting. It is better to make an error than to lose a teenager to suicide. You may experience anger from a teenager or a parent when you take such drastic action. This is a small price to pay if you rescue one adolescent. The teenager will be grateful to you at a later time. Regardless of what you do, make every attempt to get the suicidal teenager to a professional counselor as soon as possible. As a lay counselor, it isn't necessary nor in the best interest of a teenager for you to carry this type of emergency alone.

Fortunately, a youth worker is unlikely to face a seriously depressed, suicidal teenager very often. Such an experience is anxiety-provoking, even for the experienced professional. Knowing the steps that might avert a tragedy, however, can help youth workers traverse these difficult and challenging times.

Adolescent Pregnancy

There probably isn't anyone who needs the acceptance and support of a youth worker as much as a pregnant teenage girl. A young adolescent female can become pregnant a year or more following the onset of puberty. Such an event, however, places the mother and child at medical and psychological risk. In terms of the pregnant teenager, Derek Miller in his book *Attack on the Self* describes the problems this way: "The teenage mother is likely to have a preexisting emotional difficulty or to have her emotional development hindered by the experience of pregnancy. . . . A pregnant adolescent girl also is likely to experience multiple psychological stresses which impede the development of a secure sense of self. As well, the infant's needs interfere with the necessary self-involvement of the adolescent."

Adults who have worked with pregnant teenage girls realize these difficulties. About a year ago, an obviously pregnant young girl came to my office for counseling. The problems she faced are typical of young women in her same situation. She was frightened, embarrassed, and alone. The father of the child had abandoned her. He wouldn't so much as answer her phone calls. She had dropped out of school, and her friends had stopped associating with her. She was completely dependent on her nuclear family. Her mother was supportive, but her father was angry and threatening to "throw her out." At times she was angry herself. At other times she was bored. Still, at other times she was overwhelmed. I found her quite mature during several sessions, and extremely childish during others.

In the midst of all of these problems, it is the task of the youth worker to provide information and emotional support these teenagers need. Regardless of a counselor's feelings about the girl's actions, she needs acceptance and support. She is already facing the judgment of her family and friends, and many of these people on whom she normally depends for emotional support have abandoned her. In many ways, a child has been thrust into a very adult situation, with very serious consequences.

Guidelines for the Lay Counselor

Youth workers who find themselves working with a pregnant teenager will want to consider the following suggestions.

1. Communicate and demonstrate acceptance and support. The teenage girl is experiencing a high degree of stress and needs to know someone is available to her. Let her know that you value her and want to help her.

2. Talk to the girl if you suspect pregnancy. It is hard to believe, but many adolescent girls are ignorant of how conception takes place. Additionally, many pregnant girls will not recognize the signs of pregnancy unless someone else does.

3. Refer the girl to her medical doctor or a clinic to validate her pregnancy. Medical assistance is extremely important for the health of the mother and child. The sooner she has regular doctor's appointments, the better.

4. Help her tell her parents or significant others. Regardless of their initial reactions, a teenager in these circumstances needs the support of her family members. She needs your support in this process, and her parents can benefit from your calm, accepting manner regarding the situation.

5. Help the pregnant teenager find solutions to the problems she faces. For example, you might help her find out how she can continue her education. Some school districts have a special program for pregnant minors, or she might be able to attend a continuation high school or an adult education program. Perhaps you can help her get involved in a group counseling situation with other girls who are pregnant. Such a step might alleviate her isolation from young people her own age. In some cases, you might have to help her find a doctor. Her problems can be many and varied.

126

6. Use your counseling skills to help the teenager explore her feelings. A pregnant girl can feel frightened, fearful, embarrassed, ashamed, overwhelmed, depressed, guilty, angry, and confused. She needs someone with whom she can talk about her feelings regarding herself, the father, her parents, and her friends. This is a very stressful period in a pregnant girl's life, and it helps to talk about it.

7. Include the girl's family in counseling sessions. Naturally, there will be many times when you will want to work with the teenager alone. Seeing the other family members, however, can help all of the people who are impacted the most by the pregnancy. Family members may have many of the same feelings that the pregnant girl experiences.

8. Provide counsel regarding any decisions about the future of the infant. Christian families are likely to consider keeping the baby or placing it for adoption. As a youth worker, however, you may have a pregnant teenage girl in your youth group who does not come from a Christian background. Therefore, such a family may consider abortion. As a Christian youth worker, you may have very strong feelings that any abortion is morally wrong. Or, you may support abortion only in those instances of rape, incest, or when the mother's life is endangered. It appears that abortion creates greater psychological problems for adolescents than for adults. Try to counsel a family away from abortion. Remember, however, that the final decision rests with the girl and her family.

9. Accept the girl's decision regarding the future of the infant. This may be difficult if you believe she made an unwise or immoral decision. The counselor's task, however, is to communicate and demonstrate love and acceptance of the individual. Provide the teenager with the support she needs for as long as she needs it.

10. Refer the pregnant girl to a counseling professional if it appears that that would be beneficial to her. A referral can be particularly helpful if the teen's support system is quite barren.

Drug Abuse

Drug abuse has reached epidemic proportions. The situation is so serious that national leaders speak of a "War on Drugs." There is a national debate on the best way to fight this struggle. Some even view drug abuse as a threat to our national security and suggest the use of the armed forces to prevent the continued importation of drugs into the country. Much of this concern centers on the fact that more and more people, including adolescents, are becoming involved in drug use, either as users or sellers.

One of the problems in dealing with drug abuse is the fact that many people seek immediate gratification and/or relief. And the use of chemicals is one of the ways this is accomplished. There are those people, for example, who drink coffee in the morning "to get started." There are others who have a drink in the evening "to unwind." Our national motto seems to be: "I want to feel good, and I want to feel good now."

It doesn't simplify matters to realize that some harmful drugs are legal and widely available. Tobacco is a known cause of cancer, and the use of alcohol by some people becomes a progressive disease leading to death if left untreated. On the other hand, teenagers are told that other harmful drugs should not be used. The world is already complicated enough for adolescents without sending them mixed messages.

Adults who work with youth already realize the growing incidence of alcohol and illegal drug use among teenagers. Chronic alcohol and drug abuse by adolescents can impair healthy psychological, physical, and personality development. Illegal drugs interact with the central nervous system and produce artificial changes in mood, consciousness, perception, and behavior. They can lead to **tolerance,** a condition in which larger and larger doses of a drug are needed in order to produce the same results, psychological and physical dependence, and symptoms of **withdrawal,** which occur when a drug is stopped. **Dependence** is a compulsion to continue using a drug for its effects or the avoidance of ending use of a drug to prevent withdrawal symptoms. Perhaps Derek Miller says it as well as anyone: "All drug abuse is dangerous, and any use of self-prescribed, mood-changing drugs by adolescents should be a cause for concern."

Reasons for Adolescent Drug Use

Teenagers are likely to tell you that they use drugs for the effects they bring. "It makes me feel better." "I need the high." "I feel like I can do anything." "It makes me lose weight." "I feel more relaxed." All of these responses reflect the "feel good quick" philosophy of those who find it difficult to delay gratification.

Adults who work with adolescent drug abusers, however, suggest several underlying causes for drug use. First, adolescents are normally curious. They tend to try new experiences and are willing to take risks. They try different roles, wear various "costumes," and are looking for a good time with their friends. These tendencies make it easy for teenagers to experiment with drugs. The National Commission on Marijuana and Drug Abuse in 1972 defined experimental users as those who used a drug once a month or less. Although many adolescents will experiment with a drug two or three times and stop, there are many others who progress to intermittent, moderate, and/or heavy use. Some teenagers experiment with **gate-way drugs,** tobacco and alcohol, and then progress to harder drugs.

A second reason for drug abuse by adolescents has to do with their developmental process. The point has already been made that it has become more difficult to grow up due to the complexity of today's world. It is hard enough for the average teenager, but for those who are quite vulnerable and have considerably more difficulty than most, drugs can seem attractive. For example, some teenagers experience conflict between the need to be independent and the security of dependence. Separation and identity development can cause confusion, anxiety, emptiness, boredom, and depression for others. Those who display rebellious behavior (truancy, theft), isolate themselves from the adolescent mainstream, and become sexually promiscuous are more likely to use drugs than nondelinquent teenagers. The point is that teenagers having difficulty with the normal developmental process are particularly susceptible to the use of drugs.

Teenagers who self-medicate themselves provide a third apparent cause for adolescent drug abuse. The individual who feels of little value or worth, who experiences emotional deprivation, who is abused or exploited by a dysfunctional family, who feels alienated from peers, who struggles in the academic arena and/or feels overwhelmed and anxious about life may turn to drugs for relief. Taking drugs is sometimes an attempt to ease the pain, even if only temporarily.

Finally, drug use by adolescents can center on the issue of sexual development. Teenagers are exploring their sexuality, and they may experience conflicts in a variety of areas. For example, teenagers can be afraid of their sexuality, feel guilty about it, worry about impotency, fear rejection, feel anxious about homosexual thoughts. Some of these adolescents will turn to drugs to bolster their confidence and/or release tension. Some teenagers believe that drugs will enhance their sexual prowess, while others use drugs as a substitute for sex because it is less anxiety-provoking.

The underlying causes of drug abuse among adolescents suggest their particular vulnerability. They are curious, tend to experiment, and look for excitement. They also can be confused, anxious, and overwhelmed. Drug use, in spite of the advertised dangers, can seem like an easy way out for some of these young people.

Types of Drugs

Drugs that are abused by adolescents are classified into four major categories: sedatives, stimulants, hallucinogens, and the opiates. The **sedatives** include alcohol, minor tranquilizers such as Librium, Valium, and Xanex, methaqualone (Quaalude), and the barbituates (Amytal, Nembutal, Seconal, phenobarbital). Although these drugs have a sedating effect, teenagers use them because they initially produce feelings of elation and euphoria due to the fact that they suppress the inhibitory mechanisms of the brain.

Alcohol continues to be the most frequently and widely abused drug. It is widely available to teenagers, and adults appear to condone the periodic consumption of alcohol by middle and late adolescents. Commercials use youth to advertise beer, suggesting that alcohol and good times go together. A keg of beer may be provided by the parents of a teenager who is hosting a party. You might even hear a parent say, "Thank goodness it was only alcohol. That's a lot better than drugs."

Although teenagers and adults might feel good initially, sedation occurs as the amount of alcohol increases in the bloodstream. Because chronic use of alcohol leads to tolerance, increases in the amount of alcohol in order to gain the same effect can be dangerous. Increasing sedation leads to drowsiness, sleep, coma, and eventually death. In addition to tolerance, the regular use of alcohol leads to physical and psychological dependence, as well as withdrawal symptoms.

The use of methaqualone and barbituates produces similar effects to those produced by alcohol. Called "downers," "ludes," "reds," or "barbs" on the street, they produce feelings of elation and excitement initially due to the suppression of inhibitions. Many adolescents believe that the use of Qaaludes make girls more sexually available and boys more sexually potent. All of the sedatives, also known as **depressants,** lead to tolerance, physical and psychological dependence, and withdrawal symptoms. Adverse effects include slurred speech, drowsiness, impaired motor functioning, confusion, irritability, and a variety of physical symptoms. Chronic use can lead to permanent damage to the brain and other organs, and all of the sedatives can lead to sleep, coma, and death.

The **stimulants** include the amphetamines, diet pills, cocaine, and inhalants. Caffeine and nicotine, although legal and widely available, are members of this class of drugs. Teenagers use amphetamines to increase energy, to stay alert and awake, to decrease appetite, and to experience a sense of euphoria or well-being. Although it is not believed that amphetamines lead to physical dependence, chronic use results in tolerance and psychological dependence.

An amphetamine overdose can produce nausea, headaches, dizziness, confusion, apprehension, anxiety, heart palpitations, and dysphoria. Prolonged use of amphetamines can lead to an **amphetamine psychosis,** which is similar to paranoid schizophrenia. The individual in this state can experience disorganized thinking, persecutory delusions, hallucinations, as well as a variety of physical symptoms. An abrupt cessation can cause a "crash," which includes feelings of anxiety, severe depression, irritability, fatigue, and the inability to sleep. Depression can be so great that suicide can be the result. Long-term use can produce damage to the brain, heart, and lungs. Amphetamines are sometimes called "uppers," "speed," "crank," "meth," and "crystal."

Cocaine, one of the most highly publicized stimulants, produces effects similar to those produced by the amphetamines. The effects, however, last for a shorter period of time. Adolescents who can obtain and/or afford cocaine use it to enhance feelings of euphoria, excitation, perceptions of increased mental ability and strength, and to decrease appetite. Chronic users can experience those symptoms associated with an amphetamine psychosis, such as apprehension, persecutory ideation, depression, and visual and tactile hallucinations. Those individuals who overdose can experience delirium, convulsions, coma, and death. Drug abuse experts disagree as to whether cocaine produces physical dependence or tolerance, but all agree it produces psychological dependence. Cocaine is known on the street as "coke," "snow," "blow," or "flake." If it is used in a form that can be smoked, it is called "freebasing," "rock," or "crack."

Early adolescents often abuse inhalants that are found around the house. For example, they may inhale the fumes of solvents (paint thinner, glue, gasoline), and the contents from aerosol cans (spray paint, deodorants). Inhaled from a cloth, plastic bag, or other container, inhalants are used for the purpose of experiencing a "high." They can cause damage to the nervous system and other organs, affect vision, coordination, and judgment, and lead to coma and death. Users often call the inhalants "poppers," "rush," or "laughing gas."

The **hallucinogens** include LSD, PCP, and marijuana. These drugs are used to produce increased sensory awareness, visual hallucinations, changes in mood, and altered thought. Users often feel omnipotent. It appears that the effects of hallucinogens depend on the amount of dosage, the personality, experience, and expectations of the user, and the environmental clues surrounding the individual. Adverse effects include depression, anxiety, and apprehension brought on by "bad trips," delirium, and psychotic symptoms. LSD can be frightening because its effects are unpredictable, and "flashbacks" can occur after the drug is no longer being used.

PCP, also known as angel dust, is an extremely dangerous hallucinogen. Heavy and chronic use can produce a number of serious physical reactions, assaultive behavior, paranoia, depression, seizures, coma, and death. Although hallucinogens do not appear to lead to physical dependence or withdrawal symptoms, they do produce tolerance and psychological dependence.

Marijuana (cannabis) is associated with feelings of euphoria, relaxation, an altered sense of time, and heightened sensory awareness. It also decreases mental alertness, impairs memory, and reduces one's ability to concentrate. Like other hallucinogens, adverse effects of chronic marijuana use include anxiety, hallucinations, paranoia, dysphoria, withdrawal, and flashbacks. It is also believed that long-term use produces an **amotivational syndrome,** characterized by apathy, listlessness, poor judgment, lack of motivation, and decreased attention. There is some disagreement as to whether marijuana leads to tolerance, but it does lead to physical and psychological dependence, as well as withdrawal symptoms. Street names for this drug are "grass," "pot," "weed," and "hash."

The **opiates** are sedatives and painkillers. Natural opiates include opium, morphine, and codeine. All come from the opium poppy. Heroin is a derivative of morphine, and some opiates are pure synthetics (Demerol, Darvon, and methodone). Some of these opiates are used by the medical profession to inhibit pain. Drug abusers of this class of drugs, however, use them for their short-lived "rush," or a sense of euphoria, followed by a feeling of peacefulness. Chronic use leads to tolerance, physical and psychological dependence, and withdrawal symptoms.

As the dose increases, drowsiness, apathy, decreased activity, inattentiveness, impaired memory, and sleep follow. Particularly dangerous is the fact that the sedating effect of these drugs can cause slow and shallow breathing, decreased blood pressure and pulse rate, convulsions, coma, and death. If death does occur, it is usually due to respiratory failure.

Heroin is the most frequently abused opiate, producing the effects and dangers described above. It is a major cause of drug overdoses leading to death. Methodone is used by heroin users in detoxification programs. It satisfies the demands of physical dependence but does not produce the desired effects of heroin. Unfortunately, methodone is almost as addictive as heroin.

Guidelines for Lay Counselors

Due to the fact that drug users become physically and/or psychologically dependent on drugs, a teenager who is "hooked" on drugs will need professional help. They typically deny their problem, and they can manipulate and hide their drug use from anyone except well-trained and experienced drug rehabilitation counselors and other drug abusers. This does not mean that there is no counseling role for the youth worker. What it does mean is that support during and after rehabilitation is the major role of the lay counselor. Here are some guidelines to consider.

1. Talk to the teenager if you suspect drug use. Be objective and supportive. Describe the attitudes and behavior that concern

you. If the teenager is only experimenting, you may reach the individual in time to prevent further problems. For the teenager who is regularly using drugs, you may be the impetus needed for getting help.

2. Try to get the teenage drug user to make a commitment to get help. Denial is the chief defense mechanism of drug and alcohol abusers. Without an admission of the problem or a commitment to getting help, the teenager is in serious trouble.

3. Give support to the teenager's parents. Learning a son or daughter is using drugs is a parent's worst fear come true. They are likely to feel frightened, confused, guilty, angry, concerned, and overwhelmed. They need objective perspective and caring support.

4. Help the family find professional help. There are many well-trained and experienced drug rehabilitation counselors and programs. Most will tailor-make a program, and they will consider the family's resources. There is likely to be a comprehensive program for the teenager, and it will necessitate some involvement by other members of the family.

5. Continue your support of the teenager and family during the detoxification and rehabilitation period. See if you can visit the teenager in those cases where the program selected or implemented includes a residential care treatment facility. It is helpful for the teenager to feel support by someone "on the outside." For a teenager receiving help on an outpatient basis, reinforce progress of the individual.

6. Maintain your support and contact beyond the rehabilitation period. Relapses are common, and ongoing emotional support is essential for continued progress.

7. Involve the teenager in alternative activities that lessen the attraction to drugs. Help him or her develop social skills which make it easier for him or her to integrate into your youth group. Plan activities and experiences that are meaningful, relevant, interesting, and fun.

8. Continue your support in the case of a relapse. Do not take such an occurrence personally. Staying off drugs may be more difficult than getting off them. What is important is that you don't give up on a teenager.

The world of teenagers is not without its dangers — depression, suicidal thinking, teen pregnancy, and drug abuse, to name a few. Without the support of observant adults, the consequences of these dangers can be devastating and tragic for the adolescent. These evolving adults need supportive youth workers who are equipped to care.

Twelve

KNOWING
WHEN TO REFER

Every counselor has limitations. No one needs to feel as though it is necessary to handle every teenage problem that presents itself. This is true for lay counselors as well as for professional therapists. In fact, one of the most important ethical issues for psychotherapists is to determine whether or not their training and experience qualify them to work with a specific client.

When the parents of a teenager make the initial contact in regard to my seeing their son or daughter, they generally assume I will automatically accept the case if I have room in my schedule and we can find a mutually agreeable time to meet. This is not necessarily true. A part of my agenda for the initial session is to determine whether or not my qualifications will serve to help a teenager. Clients are not in my office for me. I am there for them. It is therefore unethical for me to accept a case if I do not believe I am qualified to handle the problem being presented. What every licensed profession-al realizes, including myself, is that it is impossible to have expertise in every area. A therapist might be able to help many teenagers, for example, but is not trained or experienced in counseling adolescents with eating disorders. In such cases, this licensed professional will refer the teenager to a professional who does have expertise in this area.

Youth workers who counsel teenagers are bound to face situations in which the nature of the adolescent's problem is beyond their understanding or ability to help. They need not anguish or feel guilty over this fact. This is to be expected.

The important thing is for youth workers to recognize their own strengths and weaknesses. The idea is for counselors to work with adolescents who match up with their strengths, and refer those teenagers who don't. It isn't important that any one youth worker be able to work with every teenager who has a problem. What is paramount is that the adolescent receives the kind of help needed. Sometimes a professional therapist is the "treating therapist." There are other times, however, when the role played is one of a "referring therapist." Lay counselors will find themselves in both of these roles as well. The fact that a counselor arranges for a teenager to get help is, in itself, therapeutic.

When to Refer

There are several problems presented by teenagers that are extremely serious, with potentially devastating consequences when left untreated. Youth workers can feel competent and in control when they are able to recognize quickly those young people who need to be referred to a mental health professional for an evaluation. It isn't necessary for the lay counselor to know for sure if a teenager needs to receive counseling from a professional, but it is important to know when a referral to make such a determination is advisable. Knowing when to refer will enable the youth worker to make such a recommendation with a sense of clarity and urgency. Such action on the part of the youth worker may prevent a tragedy.

It is strongly recommended that youth workers immediately refer teenagers with any of the following presenting conditions to a fully licensed, professional therapist.

1. Teenagers who are depressed. These young people feel "down," seem unhappy much of the time, and appear miserable. They have little energy, appear apathetic, and are socially withdrawn. They may display irritability, and seem overwhelmed by basic requirements of life. They seem to have little reason for living, and they feel hopeless that the future will improve for them.
2. Teenagers who are suicidal. Refer young people immediately

who talk about ending their lives, tell you it would be better if they weren't around, or verbalize they would like to go to sleep and never wake up. At times these adolescents speak as though there will be no tomorrow, or they won't be around. Sometimes they write suicide notes, or write about suicide in their journals or poetry. Suicidal teenagers often give away prized possessions, tie up loose ends, or even write a will. Because of their ambivalence, they often leave clues or write about their self-destructive feelings. Always take gestures of suicide seriously. A professional counselor will evaluate the seriousness of these signs.

3. Teenagers who use drugs. These young people need help, and they need it immediately. You need not panic, but every encounter with an illicit drug is potentially a life-threatening experience. Most drugs lead to physical dependence, and all of them lead to psychological dependence. Teenagers who use drugs need medical help and counseling in order to bring about rehabilitation.

4. Teenagers who are regularly using and/or abusing alcohol. Small amounts of alcohol may not lead to alcoholism, but alcohol is the most frequently used and widely available drug of abuse. Alcoholism among teenagers has risen dramatically, and youth workers will want to watch for signs of abuse. Particularly dangerous is the combination of alcohol and driving. In fact, the number one killer of teenagers is accidents. Remember: The use of alcohol can produce physical and psychological dependence, tolerance, and withdrawal symptoms.

5. Teenagers who appear to have an **eating disorder.** Anorexia nervosa and bulimia are rampant in our society, especially among teenage girls. Anorexia nervosa is characterized by a severe reduction in the intake of nutritional food, a failure to maintain a body weight over a minimal normal weight for height and age, an intense fear of gaining weight or being fat, disturbances in how the body is perceived, and in females, the cessation of the menstrual cycle. Teenagers who suffer from anorexia nervosa may excessively exercise, and take laxatives and diuretics. Bulimics differ in several ways, but they are best known for their pattern of binge eating, followed by the purging of food by self-induced vomiting. About one half of anorexics are also bulimic. Teenagers with these eating disorders will deny their condition. These young people need to be referred for professional counseling because their conditions are extremely complicated psychologically, and severe physical symptoms, including death, can occur if left untreated.

6. Teenagers who display psychotic behavior. Refer any young

people who think people are following them or who hear voices when the facts say otherwise. Teenagers with these symptoms are likely to be disoriented, are experiencing disordered thinking, have poor judgment, and are having difficulty interpreting the cues of their environment. They are likely to have emotional symptoms as well, such as anxiety and depression. They can become a danger to themselves and/or to others. Refer them to a licensed professional immediately.

7. Teenagers who are being neglected, abused, or sexually molested. The health, safety, and welfare of these young people are in danger. Report any suspicion of **child abuse** to a child protection agency representative in your community. You may make such a report anonymously, and you need not share your suspicions with the family if you suspect a family member to be the perpetrator. Licensed professionals are required to make such a report, and lay counselors are strongly advised to do the same.

8. Teenage girls who are pregnant. These adolescents may be alone with their secret. Therefore, they may not have had any medical attention or consultation. To ensure their health and the health of their infants, be sure they are referred to a medical doctor or clinic. Naturally, it is best if they have the support and assistance of their parents. They may need counseling in addition to a medical consultation, depending on the support they receive from their families.

9. Teenagers who are sexually active. With the outbreak of AIDS as a national epidemic, the young person who is sexually active is in grave danger. Many teenagers who engage in sexual activity do not know of its consequences. A therapist may be able to help the sexually active adolescent understand that sexual behavior is unnecessary to prove masculinity or femininity. Helping a teenager understand that sexuality is best expressed within the context of marriage is a noble task. It may also save a life.

Although the dangers may not be as imminent, youth workers are strongly advised to refer teenagers presenting the following conditions to a fully licensed counseling professional.

1. Teenagers who are acting out anger, hostility, and irresponsibility through antisocial behavior. These young people demonstrate a persistent pattern of conduct that violates the rights of others and societal norms for appropriate behavior. Their behavior is characterized by a series of incidents that includes theft, lying, shoplifting, vandalism, running away from home,

truancy, and cruelty to animals or people. These symptoms may indicate a conduct disorder that begins either in childhood or adolescence. Without treatment, these young people sometimes develop an antisocial personality disorder in adulthood.

2. Teenagers whose academic performance is consistently lower than one might expect. A variety of reasons may underlie poor performance: low self-esteem, family problems, a learning disability, poor health, the use of drugs, and depression. A trained therapist might be able to find out the underlying causes of poor performance.

3. Teenagers who have few or no friends. These adolescents present a consistent pattern of social discomfort and withdrawal from others. They refrain from getting close to others to avoid disapproval and rejection. Such behavior may be symptomatic of an avoidant or overanxious disorder.

4. Teenagers who reject the authority of their parents. Suggest a referral for an adolescent who refuses to do minimal chores, storms out of the house in a fit of anger, or displays a defiant attitude. A trained therapist may be able to uncover the underlying causes of such disruptive behavior.

Although it is strongly advised that youth workers refer teenagers for professional counseling when these conditions present themselves, there may be other times when a referral is inappropriate. The point is simple: Refer a teenager whenever the presenting problem is beyond your ability to effectively provide assistance.

To Whom Do I Refer?

Youth workers can benefit from the development of a "professional support system network." Knowing whom to call for a consultation can give the lay counselor a sense of support in an emergency. Additionally, knowing personally several competent professional counselors in private practice and being familiar with the agencies and special programs that specialize in helping teenagers with special problems can help the youth worker direct adolescents in need to those who can most effectively help them.

The following components are suggested in the development of a professional support system network.

1. Know the particulars of your community's crisis or suicide hotline. Know the services it provides, the phone number, the address, and a contact person if possible. Let a teenager in crisis know about the hotline in case you cannot be reached. Use the service yourself in the midst of a crisis if you are in need of a consultation.

2. Find out the details of national crisis hotlines if there is not a local hotline. Phone books often list toll-free numbers for emergencies. These numbers are listed under crisis, alcohol, cocaine, runaways, and drugs, among others. Make a list of these phone numbers, and keep them handy in cases of emergency.

3. Become familiar with the **child protection services** in your community or county. Know the services and procedures for obtaining help, reporting child abuse and sexual molestation cases, and referring teenagers for help.

4. Learn about the alcohol, drug, and eating disorders programs in your community or county. Knowing this information in advance can greatly benefit families in crisis. You can help them get started in finding an appropriate program for these particular problems.

5. Ask for the admission procedures and eligibility criteria for using your community or county mental health system. Sometimes these agencies are a good referral source for families. Their bureaucratic procedures can be discouraging to families in crisis, so knowing what to do in advance can have a calming effect on hurting people trying to get help.

6. Become familiar with the procedures for admitting someone to the emergency room of your local hospital. Knowing these procedures can save time and may save a teenager's life. More and more individuals are being admitted to emergency rooms for drug overdose.

7. Develop a personal relationship with several competent, licensed professional therapists in private practice. They need to be trained and experienced in working with teenagers and families. They can provide you with a consultation when you need one. Ideally, you will want to find a competent professional therapist, one who also shares your faith. This professional should be skilled in crisis intervention work, counseling teenagers with serious problems, and working with families and family systems.

Types of Professional Therapists

There are four major types of counseling professionals. They are all licensed by the state in which they practice, they have graduate-level training, they have completed significant internships under supervision, and they have successfully passed written and/or oral examinations in order to become licensed to practice psychotherapy.

Clinical Social Workers. These professionals have a graduate degree in social work, and are licensed to practice therapy. They usually have a master's degree in social work, and some hold a doctorate.

Some choose to specialize in working with adolescents and families. Clinical social workers can be found in private practice as well as in clinics and agencies.

Marriage, Family, and Child Counselors (MFCC). These counseling professionals must hold at least a master's degree in Marriage and Family Counseling or a related counseling field. Many hold the doctorate in psychology (Ph.D., Ed.D., or Psy.D.). They have completed a two-year internship, and have passed a written and an oral examination for licensure. They are specialists in problems related to communication and family dynamics. They work with adolescents and families.

Psychologists. These professionals hold a doctoral degree from a graduate program in psychology. You are likely to see a Ph.D., an Ed.D., or a Psy.D. following their names. They have completed a supervised, two-year internship, and they have completed a written and an oral examination. They work with adolescents and families. They are also trained in educational and psychological testing.

Psychiatrists. These professionals are medical doctors (M.D.), and they have specialized in psychiatry. They have had many hours of advanced study and supervised experience, much of which takes place in psychiatric hospitals. Although they work with patients in hospital settings, they also see adolescents and families in private practice settings. These are the only professionals who can prescribe medication. Many other licensed therapists consult with them when it might be advisable for a client to take medication for his or her condition. If medication is deemed advisable, it is the psychiatrist who prescribes it and monitors its effects.

Youth workers will have many opportunities to counsel teenagers who are experiencing problems that are typical for healthy, emerging adults. There will be times, however, when the problems presented by adolescents will be serious enough to warrant professional assistance by licensed psychotherapists. Knowing when to refer and to whom increases the effectiveness of the youth worker. In some cases, the endangered lives of teenagers will be spared.

Thirteen

TAKING
CARE OF YOURSELF

Counselors accompany those who are confused, hurting, and stagnant. They facilitate clarity, healing, and growth. They provide knowledge, skill, and support. They make themselves available, but they wait until invited by those who desire their help. They stay involved for as long as they are needed and for as long as they can contribute to the healthy development of the person in need. The source of their fulfillment is the client's growth.

Youth workers who counsel adolescents face a challenge of immense proportions. At the very time when teenagers are fighting hard for independence, these caring adults offer to provide "an assist." When these young people are trying to create distance from significant adults, lay counselors are trying to get close. As these emerging adults are trying to define identity on their own, these supportive youth leaders are trying to provide reinforcement. The process, however, is a tenuous one. Teenagers can bolt from counseling at any moment, and they often do. And just about the time a counselor thinks an adolescent is no longer interested, the teenager returns for continued help.

This act of "coming alongside" these somewhat fragile adolescents can be tremendously satisfying and fulfilling. It can also be frustrating and energy depleting. The more involved a youth worker becomes in counseling teenagers, the more cumulative its effects. Those who counsel adolescents over a long period of time can experience symptoms of burnout: loss of energy, working harder but accomplishing less, losing interest in the process, feeling de-energized, loss of confidence in ability, feeling trapped, and depression.

Psychologists describe human beings as a "closed energy system." This concept suggests that each of us has a limited supply of energy. In other words, we have a fixed amount of energy available to us. When it is depleted, it must be regained. To disregard this characteristic is to flirt with danger. In extreme cases, suicide can be the consequence of the caring professional who goes beyond a present energy reserve. It is imperative that counselors take care of themselves. Otherwise, they become of no use to others or to themselves.

I have always been impressed with the fact that Jesus placed a high priority on the need to regain energy. His days were often heavily scheduled, He spoke to hundreds of people, and He became intimately involved in the struggles of others. At the end of a busy day, He would often tell His disciples to meet him on the other side of the lake. He guarded His need for solitude and time when He didn't have to respond to others by carving out time alone. Even when He would pray, He would ask His very closest associates to wait a distance from the site of His praying. He knew the limits of His energy and resources, and He worked within them.

There is no doubt that each counselor is unique in terms of those activities that serve to re-energize. What is energizing to one counselor may not be energizing to another. For some, rest and relaxation are the key. Others are more interested in projects or activities. Most counselors probably seek a variety of activities which provide both rest and stimulation. Lay counselors will need to be actively involved in their own process of determining and establishing a program that brings a sense of health and well-being. Learning how to take care of yourself is of the utmost importance. It is impossible to care for another when you don't know how to take care of yourself.

Strategies for Recovery

It is very helpful to recognize your own energy pattern and work within it. Some individuals are similar to those big workhorses used on farms. They are slow and plodding, but they are able to carry a big work load. Other individuals are more like thoroughbred race horses. They are fast and efficient, but they rest often. In my own case, I counsel full-time for two days, rest one day, counsel full-time for two more days, and then rest over the weekend. For years I counseled four days in a row and then rested for three days. My ability to sustain the counseling process for so many days in a row is no longer possible. I need breaks more often in order to have the kind of energy necessary to help people through their struggles.

Typically, youth workers do not counsel teenagers on a full-time basis. These adults play many roles, and counseling is but one mode of interaction they have with growing adolescents. The patterns of work determined by youth workers, therefore, will be very different from the pattern I have evolved. Youth workers, however, need to recognize their own energy patterns and work within them.

Most professional counselors realize the benefits of a physical fitness program. Staying physically fit helps to increase and maintan one's level of health, which in turn has a positive effect on one's emotionality. Running, jogging, walking, aerobics, and working out can all increase the energy level of a counselor.

Another way to regain energy is to learn to play along the way. Parents usually teach their children that they may play after the work is done. Play, rest, and relaxation is therefore presented as a reward for a job well done. Unfortunately for most adults, including counselors, our work is never done. Certainly the development of teenagers is a continuous and nonstop process. If counselors were to wait to play until the work is completed, they would never be able to play.

The key for counselors, then, is to learn to play along the way. For example, perhaps a counselor is energized by teaching and de-energized by counseling. Teaching and counseling can be integrated in such a way that the "play" of teaching can provide the energy necessary for counseling. A lay counselor may want to integrate these two functions by counseling teenagers and teaching a seminar to parents on the healthy development of adolescents.

The blending of work and play doesn't have to be formal. I used to work in an office that was on the edge of a river. The river's banks were green and lush with foliage. It teemed with wildlife right in the heart of the city. The setting always reminded me of my carefree, youthful days growing up in a small California town.

Several times each day, following a number of counseling sessions, I would close my door, open the drapes and look out on the river. Instantly, I was once again a little boy, free from adult responsibilities, playing alongside the river. I was always able to begin counseling again, refreshed and completely energized. Learn to play along the way, or you won't play at all.

It can also be very beneficial to actively look for health, growth, and development. It is easy to focus on the struggles, the dysfunction, the blocks to growth. To become immersed in the difficulties of others means that we share these problems. Like everyone else, however, counselors need periodic encouragement. Hurting, confused people do not encourage the counselor. Youth workers must therefore learn to find clues in the environment that tell them they are doing a good job.

Suppose you are working with a depressed young teenage boy. At the end of one of your counseling sessions, he casually tells you that he is going to his school's football game on Friday night with a friend of his. This announcement might not seem very significant to the casual observer. In fact, this teenager might not even realize the positive implications of his plans. As counselors, however, we realize that depressed teenagers tend to withdraw from their friends. They lose interest in activities around them and they don't want to be a burden to their friends.

The fact that this young adolescent is planning to attend a game with a friend is great news! Without making a big deal about this young man's news, the counselor would quietly celebrate the moment. Indications that our work is successful and helpful are very energizing and fulfilling to those of us who work with teenagers. But we will have to look for these clues in order to find them.

It is always important to remind yourself that the problems of counselees belong to them. Counselors are people, and they have problems of their own. To take on the problems of others as though they are your own taxes your limits and leads to overload. Counselors who take on the problems of their clients cannot leave their work at the office. Instead, they carry these burdens wherever they go. They even take them home, and they are present when the adolescent is absent. They never get a break from this heavy load.

On occasion, I have told a few of my clients that they can expect me to make every attempt to be fully present during a counseling session. I will try to keep my mind from wandering, and I will make every effort to focus on them and them alone. Such a task becomes increasingly difficult as we become overloaded with all the problems of our counselees. We need to be able to set aside the problems that truly belong to others in order to enable us to rest and recover. Interestingly, the word **relationship** means the ability to connect again and again. It isn't necessary for us to be connected with another person continuously in order to have a meaningful relationship. What is important is that we have the ability to connect repeatedly when we come in contact with another person. The period of "disconnection" enables us to regain our own sense of self as well as our energy. This in turn enables us to be fully present when "reconnecting" with a teenager during a counseling session.

Another way to take care of yourself is to make sure you address your own needs. It is more likely that we can help others when we are full than when we are empty. Several years ago, a psychologist from Oregon, Sterling Ellsworth, made a statement I have never forgotten. He was addressing a group of teachers at a meeting prior to the start of the new school year. He said, "If you expect to fill your kids' love buckets, your own needs to be full." He was suggesting that we can't give something to another if we have nothing to give.

Counselors need to be aware of their own needs and respect them as valid. Do you need to set aside time to develop your own adult relationships? Very often youth workers become alienated and distant from other adults because they are with teenagers most of the time. Are you struggling with your own sense of identity? Have you given yourself away so often that you have lost touch with who you are? Maybe you need to spend some time getting your feet back on the ground so that you don't get lost when working with confused teenagers. Perhaps you feel spiritually empty and need to renew your relationship with God. Are you experiencing a conflict with another colleague but have not had the time to confront the problem? If so, it is likely to be draining your energy from the tasks you need to accomplish. The needs of counselors are similar to other adults, and the wise counselor gives the necessary attention to meeting them.

Doing something different or unexpected is a fairly easy way to stimulate renewal and recovery. I know a pastor who used to take vacations in the same city in which he lived and worked! He lived in a city in which thousands of tourists arrive each year to enjoy the scenery, climate, and tourist attractions. He realized that hard-working people from other cities came to his city for rest and relaxation. So he and his wife would annually reserve a room in one of the local hotels, and they would enjoy "being away from it all."

Due to the nature of my work as a professional therapist, my work days are completely scheduled. When I go to work I know what I will be doing, and who I will see. There is nothing wrong with planning my days in advance. In fact, it's necessary that I do so. But routine and careful scheduling reduces the joy of spontaneity. I therefore make every attempt to approach my day off at midweek without having anything scheduled in advance. I want to get up, take a reading of my needs, and spontaneously decide how I want to spend the time. This spontaneity provides a departure from the usual, the routine. And this departure from my regular activities as a counselor stimulates my energy, and makes it easier to return to my counseling.

Remember to work within your areas of expertise. In an earlier chapter, we spoke of the fact that every counselor has limitations in knowledge and skill. We mentioned this in the context of ethics. It is unethical to suggest to a client that we can deliver in an area in which we have little experience or expertise. In the context of this chapter, however, it is tremendously exhausting to attempt something about which we have little interest, confidence, or natural ability. On the other hand, one's energy level is high when we are involved in something we enjoy and can do well.

Naturally, there are some areas in which we have little experience but high interest. Learning these kinds of new skills can be energizing and stimulating. There are other areas, however, that do not fit our personality, our style, or our strengths. In the mental health field, for example, psychologists have traditionally used psychological tests to help them assess and evaluate clients. In order to be licensed, they must demonstrate their ability and knowledge regarding psychological testing. In practice, however, there are a signficant number of these professionals who do not feel comfortable testing other people as a means of gathering information. Frankly, they dislike testing and find the process something they would rather have others do for them. So they refer their clients to other professionals who enjoy the process of assessment, and they spend their professional time involved in other activities of the counseling process. Referring a teenager to another person who is better prepared to help with a specific problem is not only in the best interest of that teenager, but it serves to help a counselor preserve energy for use in other, more appropriate areas.

Counselors who take care of themselves recognize the importance of developing a personal support system. It it generally believed that individuals need to be a part of a group after they have arrived at an acceptable level of health and well-being. Interestingly, there is research that suggests that it is the creative, nourishing, supportive group that provides what individuals need to maintain health!

Many professional counselors choose to work within the context of a group, clinic, or agency. When you talk to many of these individuals, you begin to recognize that they do not want to practice counseling in isolation from others. They need and seek out other professionals with which to work. For a number of years, I have not only worked within the context of a group, but I regularly have lunch with my colleagues. Sometimes we talk about "the business," but more likely we are simply enjoying a sense of collegiality.

By the very nature of counseling, individuals who counsel others demonstrate their strength in an affiliative way. They find themselves helping, supporting, advising, counseling. They are usually sharing their strength with others. The benefit of a support group is that the members share their strength with the counselor. What we notice is that the strength of others often stimulates one's own energy reserve. This is the secret of conventions. As counselors talk to other counselors, they "borrow" their strength, their excitement, their energy. They become energized and ready to return to work.

Consciously recognize that being a counselor defines what you do, not who you are. Counselors need to hang up their counseling hat when they "leave the office." The process of counseling is hard work, and counselors simply cannot be "at work" all the time. There are other roles that are just as important as the counseling role. But, these are roles only. The basis for a counselor's strength begins with one's personhood. The counselor who takes care of this personhood is more likely to recover from the de-energizing nature of the roles that are played.

Protecting one's person is sometimes very challenging. Once someone knows you are a counselor, they attempt to place you in that role continuously. It doesn't seem to matter to them that you may need a break from what you do. They will ask you for professional advice wherever they find you. Learning to respond to these advances as a friend rather than as a counselor will help to keep you in touch with you and who you are. And, learning to leave your work at the office is another way to conserve energy.

Finally, pray for God's strength and resources as you counsel teenagers. The task is too great to depend on your own strength. Each day before you begin your work, ask God for His strength, wisdom, and will for your life as you begin the task of helping teenagers develop into mature adulthood. Catherine Marshall describes in great detail the work of the Holy Spirit in her little book called *The Helper.* She reminds us of the power that God can supply us with through the work of the Spirit.

Some days we simply wonder how we will manage to be helpful to adolescents who are trying their best to find their way. The only direction for guidance is to look heavenward. We can rejoice on those days when we realize that the energy we are using is coming from a source other than our own. We can be grateful for God's care, love, and support for us.

It is a privilege to counsel teenagers. They only allow a few adults to participate so directly in their growth and development. Their invitation to do so suggests a great deal of trust in a counselor. Youth leaders who counsel these young people can protect this trust by equipping themselves to effectively care for these emerging, evolving adults.

This task of counseling adolescents is a significant, challenging one. There are no easy answers to the very difficult questions teenagers face. That's why counseling can be tiring, if not exhausting at times. Counselors who neglect themselves reduce their effectiveness. Taking care of yourself not only provides the energy you need to assist teenagers to grow and develop, but it will provide them with a model for valuing themselves.

Teenagers demand our best. As counselors, we had best not give them less.

Glossary

This glossary is composed of the most important terms and expressions found in the text. The definitions are for the purpose of providing youth workers with a quick grasp of key concepts needed to understand the counseling process.

accurate empathic understanding   The process of understanding another person's subjective experience.

active crisis state   The stage of a crisis in which an individual experiences a sense of disequilibrium, feelings of panic, inadequacy, and hopelessness. Physical and emotional symptoms are present, and thoughts of suicide may develop.

active listening   A form of listening in which the listener is fully involved with what is being communicated by the speaker.

adolescence   A term which is used to identify the period between the onset of puberty and adulthood.

advising   A form of interaction in which one person suggests alternative solutions to the problems of another.

affirmation   A counseling technique in which the counselor authentically expresses the value and esteem in which the counselee is held.

age-appropriate   Characteristics or behavior patterns that are typical and normal for individuals within a particular age-span.

amotivational syndrome   Symptoms produced by prolonged use of marijuana. They include apathy, listlessness, lack of motivation, poor judgment, and decreased attention.

amphetamine psychosis   Symptoms which are similar to paranoid schizophrenia that result from the prolonged use of amphetamines.

blended family   A family in which the married adults have been married previously and have brought children from previous marriages. The new family must be blended together in order to make a cohesive unit.

child abuse   Abusive behavior is defined by the laws of each state but includes the neglect, sexual molestation, physical and/or emotional abuse of children.

child care custodians   Employees of public and private schools, child-care or day-care centers, residential-care facilities, and group homes; social workers; probation officers; and foster parents.

child protection services   Public agencies which are given responsibility for ensuring the health, safety, and welfare of children. Probation and welfare departments, and local law enforcement agencies are examples.

clinical social worker   A mental health professional who holds a graduate degree in social work and is licensed to practice psychotherapy.

cognitive therapy   A counseling approach that helps the counselee develop more positive thought patterns. This approach has proven to be successful in the treatment of depression.

concrete operations   One of the stages of intellectual development. Children in this stage, who are between the ages of 7 and 12, are able to organize facts, understand classification systems, and do concrete problems.

confidentiality   A term that refers to a standard of professional conduct regarding the disclosure of information. A licensed counselor may not disclose information obtained in the course of counseling without the permission of the counselee.

confrontation   A counseling technique used by counselors to encourage a counselee to face inconsistencies and issues which have been denied or repressed.

congruence   The authentic, spontaneous, and genuine expression of one's internal response to another person.

contract   A counseling strategy in which an agreement is developed which defines a counselee's expected behavior.

conventional level   The second level of Kohlberg's stages of moral development. This is usually the stage at which early adolescents may be found. They are interested in behavior that results in the approval of others.

counseling   A process in which an individual explores issues, resolves conflicts, makes decisions, and changes dysfunctional behavior patterns by working with a counselor.

countertransference   A situation in which a counselor unconsciously and inappropriately displaces onto a counselee behavior patterns and emotional reactions more appropriate to a relationship with a significant other.

crisis   A temporary state in which individuals face obstacles that are impossible to surmount by their usual methods of problem-solving.

crisis intervention   The process in which a counselor takes whatever steps are necessary to help an individual resolve a crisis.

dependence   A condition in which an individual compulsively continues to abuse a drug for its effects or in order to avoid withdrawal symptoms.

depressant   A chemical that acts on the central nervous system. Depressants are abused because they initially produce feelings of elation due to the suppression of inhibitory mechanisms of the brain. The use of these drugs leads to tolerance, physical and psychological dependence, and withdrawal symptoms. Examples are alcohol, minor tranquilizers, methaqualone, and the barbituates. An overdose of these drugs can lead to sleep, coma, and death. Depressants are also known as sedatives.

depression   An emotional disorder which is characterized by a depressed mood, loss of energy, eating and/or sleeping disturbances, social withdrawal, loss of interest, a sense of hopelessness, irritability, and/or suicidal thoughts.

diagnosis   The counselor's determination of a counselee's problem.

door opener   Pattern of communication which tends to encourage a counselee to talk.

duty to report   When the law requires specific individuals to disclose information related to particular circumstances. Licensed counselors, for example, must report any suspicion or evidence of child abuse.

eating disorder   Grossly disordered eating patterns. Anorexia nervosa and bulimia are examples of eating disorders.

egocentrism   The inability to view life from an objective point of view. Teenagers define most everything in terms of what it means to them.

evaluative statement   A counseling technique in which the counselor shares a judgment regarding a counselee's behavior.

experiential   Learning by doing. The learner actually experiences that which is to be learned.

extended family   A nuclear family plus other relatives such as grandparents, aunts, uncles, and cousins who live together or in close proximity.

follow up   A step in the counseling process in which the counselor checks on the progress of the counselee after the counseling relationship has been terminated.

formal operations   The stage of intellectual development that begins in early adolescence and is characterized by the ability to think logically and abstractly.

formulation   The first step of crisis intervention counseling in which the counselor seeks to find out what happened, assesses the individual's response, and evaluates the potential dangers.

gateway drugs   Drugs such as tobacco and alcohol that sometimes lead to the use of illegal drugs.

hallucinogens   Drugs of abuse which produce increased sensory awareness, visual hallucinations, changes in mood, and altered thought patterns. LSD, PCP, and marijuana are examples of this class of drugs. The use of PCP leads to tolerance and psychological dependence, and an overdose can lead to seizures, coma, and death. The use of marijuana leads to physical and psychological dependence, as well as withdrawal symptoms.

hazardous event   The first stage of a crisis. It is an event that is extremely threatening or stressful to an individual.

holder of the privilege   The individual who must give permission to disclose information gained in the course of counseling.

homework assignment   Tasks, exercises, and practice activities that are given to a family for the purpose of reinforcing something that has been learned in a family counseling session.

identity   The integration of various aspects of the self into a coherent, unified, acceptable sense of self.

implementation   The second step in crisis intervention in which the counselor puts into practice the intervention plan and focuses on the steps necessary to resolve the crisis.

individuation   The development and awareness of a person as a unique individual.

individuative-reflective faith   One of the stages of faith development. It is the stage in which one's faith is defined in a very personal term. Only the most mature adolescents can be found in this stage of faith development.

interpretation   A counseling technique used to explore the possible motives and meanings of an individual's behavior.

interview   The term given to a counseling session by psychiatrists and psychologists.

labile   A term used to describe unpredictable and changing emotions.

marriage, family, and child counselor   A licensed counselor who holds a graduate degree in marriage, family, and child counseling; and who specializes in communication and relationship problems.

nuclear family   A set of parents and their children.

opiates   Drugs of abuse that are sedatives and pain killers. Opium and heroin are drugs in this classification. Chronic use leads to tolerance, physical and psychological dependence, and withdrawal symptoms. An overdose can lead to convulsions, coma, and death.

passive listening   This form of listening is also known as silence.

pluralistic society A society in which diverse views and behavior are present and tolerated.

preaching A form of interaction in which a person attempts to influence another person to accept or reject an idea or truth.

precipitating factor One of the stages of a crisis. It is an event that ushers in an active crisis state.

prescription A technique used in family counseling. It is a set of instructions given to the family by the counselor.

presenting problem The initial reason given by a counselee for initiating counseling.

principled level The third level of Kohlberg's stages of moral development. Only the most highly developed teenagers in late adolescence reach this level. For those who do, behavior is based on principles, whether or not personal gain is achieved.

privileged communication The legal right to prevent information gained in the course of counseling to be used in a court of law.

probing A counseling technique that encourages an individual to explore more deeply his thoughts, feelings, and behavior.

psychiatrist A medical doctor who specializes in psychiatry. Psychiatrists are the only mental health professionals who can prescribe medication.

psychologist A mental health professional who holds a doctorate in psychology and is licensed to practice psychotherapy. Psychologists are specialists in educational and psychological testing.

psychopathology The study of psychological and behaviorial dysfunctions which occur in mental disorders.

puberty Sexual maturity.

pubescence Changes that occur in late childhood or early adolescence leading to sexual maturity of the individual.

questioning A counseling technique used to gather information from a counselee.

rapping Informal talks or discussions held by teenagers.

reality test The process in which a counselee compares his perceptions of the truth with what is actually true.

reflection A counseling technique in which the counselor expresses the counselee's point of view.

reintegration The final state of crisis intervention counseling in which the person in crisis returns to a state of equilibrium.

relationship   The ability to connect emotionally with another person again and again.

role playing   A counseling strategy in which a counselee is requested to play the role of a significant other.

sculpting   A counseling technique used in family counseling in which an individual arranges family members in a way that expresses the dynamics or relationship patterns of the family.

sedatives   See depressant.

self-disclosure   The act of sharing one's "inside self" with another.

separation   A term used to describe a teenager's tendency to distance from parents for the purpose of developing one's own identity.

silence   A counseling technique used to encourage an individual to continue to work through an issue without being interrupted by the counselor.

stimulants   Drugs of abuse which are used to increase energy, alertness, and a sense of euphoria. Stimulants include amphetamines, diet pills, cocaine, and inhalants. Prolonged use of amphetamines produces tolerance and psychological dependence. Cocaine overdose can produce delirium, convulsions, coma, and death.

strategies   The ideas which are implemented in order to reach a counseling goal.

suicidal ideation   Having suicidal or self-destructive thoughts or ideas.

suicidal intent   Having the purpose of committing suicide.

synthetic-conventional faith   One of the stages of faith development. Most teenagers are at this stage of their development of faith. Their faith is defined in terms of their interpersonal relationships.

system   A family counseling term which describes the fact that individuals influence and are influenced by the family as a whole. The individual is a part, and the family is viewed as a whole. The system approach is one of the major reasons for seeing an entire family in counseling.

talk therapy   Therapy that relies on a counselor and counselee talking about issues, conflicts, and necessary changes in dysfunctional behavior patterns.

teaching   An interaction mode in which one person shares his knowledge, experience, and expertise with another.

techniques   Methods used by counselors to effect growth and development of the individual in counseling.

termination The final step in a course of counseling in which the counselor and counselee agree that the goals of counseling have been met.

therapeutic alliance A relationship in which a counselor and counselee agree to work toward a counseling goal on behalf of the counselee.

tolerance A condition in drug users in which larger and larger doses of a drug are needed to produce the desired results.

traditional family A family in which the marriage of the husband and wife is the first and only marriage of either; they are the biological parents of all the children in the home; the father works outside the home and the mother works in the home.

transference The counselee unconsciously and inappropriately displaces onto the counselor behavior patterns or emotional reactions more appropriate to a relationship with a significant other.

treatment plan A plan devised by a counselor, complete with component parts, which will be implemented to help a counselee reach a counseling goal.

unconditional positive regard Deep caring for another person that is not contingent upon that person's thoughts, feelings, or behavior.

vulnerable state The second stage of a crisis. It is the individual's reaction to a stressful event.

withdrawal Physical and psychological symptoms which occur when a drug is withdrawn.

Bibliography

Bateson, G., D.O. Jackson, J. Haley, and J. Weakland. "Toward a Theory of Schizophrenia." *Behavioral Science,* 1956: 1(4), pp. 251–264.

Boyer, Patricia and Ronald Jeffrey. *A Guide for the Family Therapist.* New York: Jason Aronson, Inc., 1984.

Buntman, Peter and E.M. Saris. *How to Live with Your Teenager.* Pasadena, Calif.: The Birch Tree Press, 1979.

Burns, David. *Feeling Good: The New Mood Therapy.* New York: Signet Books, 1980.

Caplan, G. *An Approach to Community Mental Health.* New York: Grune and Stratton, 1961.

Coles, Robert and Geoffrey Stokes. *Sex and the American Teenager.* New York: Harper and Row, 1985.

Combs, A.W., D.L. Avila, and W.W. Purkey. *Helping Relationships: Basic Concepts for the Helping Professions.* Boston: Allyn and Bacon, 1971.

Combs, A.W., et. al. *Florida Studies in the Helping Professions.* University of Florida Social Science Monograph, 1969, No. 37.

Committee on Child Psychiatry. *The Process of Child Therapy.* New York: Brunner/Mazel Publishers, 1982.

Corey, Gerald, ed. *Theory and Practice of Counseling and Psychotherapy.* Monterey, California: Brooks/Cole Publishing Company, 1977.

Dodson, Laura and DeWayne Kurpius. *Family Counseling: A Systems Approach.* Muncie, Indiana: Accelerated Development, 1977.

Elkind, David. *The Hurried Child: Growing Up Too Fast Too Soon.* Reading, Mass.: Addison-Wesley Publishing Company, 1981.

Erikson, Erik H. *Identity: Youth and Crisis.* New York: W.W. Norton Company, 1968.

Fowler, James W. *Stages of Faith: The Psychology of Human Development and the Quest for Meaning.* San Francisco, California: Harper and Row, 1981.

Golan, Naomi. *Treatment in Crisis Situations.* New York: The Free Press, 1978.

Gordon, Thomas. *Parent Effectiveness Training.* New York: Peter H. Wyden, Inc., 1970.

Haley, Jay. *Uncommon Therapy: The Psychiatric Techniques of Milton H. Erickson, M.D.* New York: Norton, 1973.

Hollis, F. *Casework: A Psychosocial Therapy.* New York: Random House, 1972.

James, Jennifer. "Directions for Change." Speech delivered to the California Media and Library Educators Association Convention in San Diego, California, 1985.

Joan, Polly. *Preventing Teenage Suicide: The Living Alternative Handbook.* New York: Human Sciences Press, Inc., 1985.

Jourard, Sidney M. *The Transparent Self: Self-Disclosure and Well-Being,* 2nd ed., New York: D. Van Nostrand Company, 1971.

Kohlberg, Lawrence. "Stage and Sequence: The Cognitive-Developmental Approach to Socialization." In D.A. Goslin (Ed.), *Handbook of Socialization Theory and Research.* Chicago: Rand McNally, 1969.

L'Abate, Luciano, et. al. *Methods of Family Therapy.* Englewood Cliffs, New Jersey: Prentice-Hall, 1986.

L'Amour, Louis. *Ride the Dark Trail.* New York: Bantam Books, 1972.

Lefrancois, Guy R. *Of Children.* Belmont, California: Wadsworth Publishing, 1973.

Littwin, Susan. *The Postponed Generation.* New York: William Morrow & Company, Inc., 1987.

MacKinnon, Roger and Robert Michels. *The Psychiatric Interview in Clinical Practice.* Philadelphia: W.B. Saunders Company, 1971.

Marshall, Catherine. *The Helper.* New York: Avon Books, 1978.

McGoldrick, Monica and Elizabeth A. Carter. "The Family Life Cycle." In F. Walsh (Ed.), *Normal Family Processes.* New York: Guilford Press, 1982.

Miller, Derek. *Attack on the Self: Adolescent Behavioral Disturbances and Their Treatment.* Northvale, N.J.: Jason Aronson Inc., 1986.

Mussen, Paul H., et. al. *Psychological Development: A Life-Span Approach.* New York: Harper and Row, 1979.

Nichols, William C. and Craig A. Everett. *Systemic Family Therapy: An Integrative Approach.* New York: The Guilford Press, 1986.

Olson, G. Keith. *Counseling Teenagers.* Loveland, Colo.: Group Books, 1984.

Peck, M. Scott. *The Different Drum: Community Making and Peace.* New York: Simon and Schuster, 1987.

Peck, M. Scott. *The Road Less Traveled.* New York: Simon and Schuster, 1978.

Piaget, Jean. *The Psychology of Intelligence.* London: Routledge and Kegan Paul, 1950.

Pittman III, Frank S. *Turning Points: Treating Families in Transition and Crisis.* New York: W.W. Norton and Company, 1987.

Rogers, Carl R. *On Becoming a Person.* Boston: Houghton Mifflin, 1961.

Rowley, William J. *Nothing to Hide.* Wheaton, Ill.: Victor Books, 1989.

Schultz, Stephen. *Family Systems Therapy: An Integration.* New York: Jason Aronson, Inc., 1984.

Shostrom, Everett L. *Manual for the Personal Orientation Inventory.* San Diego, Calif.: Educational and Industrial Testing Service, 1966.

Vital Statistics in the United States (1960–1980). *Mortality Rate Part B.*

Williams, A.L. *All You Can Do Is All You Can Do But All You Can Do Is Enough.* New York: Oliver-Nelson, 1988.

Wolberg, Lewis R. *Handbook of Short-Term Psychotherapy.* New York: Thieme-Stratton, 1980.